L

FOUND ME

Exploring the unconscious movements of desire - how they form us, connect us, shape our greatest ideas, mold our societies, influence human history and ultimately, how they are unveiled.

BY ANDRÉ RABE

2

© 2014 Andre Rabe. All rights reserved.
ISBN: 978-0-9931554-0-6
Published by Andre Rabe Publishing.

Cover artwork by Mary-Anne Rabe.

Scriptural quotations are taken from a wide variety of translations. Each quotation includes the relevant reference to the translation used.

CONTENTS

INTRODUCTION   4

PART 1 - REFLECTIVE HUMAN NATURE

1 - ENCOUNTER THE MYSTERY   12
2 - MORE THAN MYSELF   18
3 - DESIRE FOUND ME   36
4 - DESIRING YOUR NEIGHBOR'S ASS   56

PART 2 - DEVELOPING STORIES

5 - REFLECTIVE LANGUAGE   84
6 - SCRIPTURE CONVERSING WITH MYTH   98
7 - MYSTERY OF GOD   128
8 - STORY OF SACRIFICE   152
9 - PARADOX OF EVIL   166
10 - HISTORY OF SATAN   176
11 - COMING MESSIAH   184

PART 3- REDEFINED

12 - HISTORY SUMMARIZED IN HIS STORY   198
13 - ZOMBIE APOCALYPSE!?   230
15 - ATONEMENT THEORIES AND SACRIFICE   272
16 - MIMETIC AT-ONE-MENT   294
17 - BEAUTIFUL CONTRASTS   324
RECOMMENDED READING   340

INTRODUCTION

Writing this book took a few years longer than what I first anticipated. Previous books seemed to simply happen; compiling them was a quick process of organizing my thoughts and meditations into a logical written format. But something very different happened during the writing of *Desire Found Me*. I discovered something; an idea had taken root and was spreading through all my previously held beliefs. The process and logic with which I used to approach topics started falling apart when applied to this discovery. With great frustration I eventually realized that I was not dealing with just another topic, another set of concepts, another perspective, but rather, with the essence that connects them all. As such no one concept or perspective could ever adequately describe it. God and our concepts of God are not identical. God seldom, if ever, reveals concepts about himself. He simply reveals himself. Such encounters deeply transform our concepts.

In 2010 Mary-Anne and I began traveling much more extensively for speaking engagements. Most weekends we ministered in churches and during the week our appointments were with small groups… which meant that instead of speaking to a well-behaved, quiet audience, people spoke back! Some even questioned the profound wisdom we were sharing with them! Very soon the nature of these engagements were transformed into honest conversations rather than the kind of monologues that we are familiar with in traditional religious settings. Often we would have more than seven such appointments per week. We seldom stayed in hotels but were welcomed into local homes. In the process we discovered new friends, brothers, sisters and parents. We found ourselves involved in new communities, participating in their joys and sorrows, struggling with relevant questions and celebrating new discoveries together.

No concept was considered too sacred to question. These communities were much more interested in reality than religion. What a joy to find beauty, not only in the abstract but in the midst of real lives, real circumstances, real faces. We found that the form of truth is not restricted to an inner experience but is surprisingly tangible in relationship. In the middle of all this busyness and interaction with people, we sensed how the Word becomes flesh, how God is found in every true encounter. The wisdom, the insights and the learning of these new friends enriched us beyond description. The very pertinent questions we faced inspired us to study afresh. Countless flights and sleepless nights in different time-zones became ideal opportunities to read, write and explore further. It was during this time that a well-read friend (thanks Tito) introduced me to the writings of René Girard. Mistakenly I purchased the first book I found by him in electronic form. It was the book *Sacrifice* and I do not suggest it as a first introduction to Girardian thinking. However, I glimpsed something that motivated me to get some of his other works. Over the few years that followed it became a huge contribution to my own understanding and I must have read more than a hundred books specifically exploring René Girard's Mimetic Realism.

The form of truth began to change from abstract theories into something much more real - that which makes us true. It was the philosopher Spinoza who said that men consider themselves free, because they are conscious of their decisions and their desires, but they remain ignorant of (and therefore in bondage to) the influences that cause them. How true. The essence of our lives, the deep movements that make us human, are deeper than our beliefs. What we believe is just one way in which we try to unveil these movements in a more visible form. Uncovering these unconscious movements that form us is a risk... a risk to who we thought we were, a risk to all we thought we knew. If this sounds frightening, it should. But it is also exciting. Risk exposes us to both danger and opportunity.

Declaring your love for the one who captured your heart might be the start of a lifelong romance... or the end of your joyful and naive little heart! But you will never know unless you take the risk. Yes, you could avoid the potential pain, but in doing so you also avoid the joy of living, for living without risk is the most boring existence. Some of the greatest risks you can ever expose yourself to are facing your hidden beliefs, purposely becoming conscious of your unconscious assumptions and discovering the desires that energize you. These are the ultimate risks, for in doing so you might just lose yourself... and find another self you hardly knew.

This book, therefore, does not intend to simply confirm what you already believe. This book is a risk. A risk to your current state of mind, a risk to some of your deeply held beliefs and as such a risk to who you think you are.

For those of you brave enough to open yourselves up to risk, I trust that in doing so you will discover a God who is open to risk as well, a God who desires and a God who allows himself to be deeply affected by us. When we let go of our stale and set dogmas, we begin to glimpse a God who is not stagnant but dynamically responsive to us, engaged in relevant life-giving conversation. This God has no desire to manipulate or control but has given himself completely into the hands of his creation. He is indeed the God of infinite possibilities.

8

It is my desire that through the words in this book you would receive more than words, that you would encounter the presence of beauty, the mystery of self-giving love.

Part 1 - Reflective Human Nature

1 - ENCOUNTER THE MYSTERY

"Would you like to hike in France with me for a couple of weeks?" Mary-Anne asked me. I was delighted as I generally enjoy activity more than conversation. I would much rather do a hike with a friend and along the way share the experience of a beautiful landscape than sit in a lounge and discuss the beauty of nature. And so, a few years ago Mary-Anne, Eugene (our son), and I hiked the French portion of the Camino de Santiago for a couple of weeks. Every day consisted of about 9 hours of walking with a pack that was far too heavy as I was stupid enough to have brought books and electronics that were never needed. However, I have never enjoyed food and rest and anything that resembled a bed as much as during those few weeks. The views along the way were spectacular. There were mountain tops and landscapes that could not be accessed any other way but via these footpaths. The difficulty of the walk was soon forgotten when rewarded with such sights, or with the water from a cool spring, or a hearty meal at the end of the day.

Participating in reality is much more exiting than a second-hand account of a fading memory. This, for me, is the greatest challenge with the journey we are about to embark on. I have no intention of boring you with lifeless theories; together with you I want to hike the most challenging, yet beautiful terrain our minds are capable of. There are certain experiences, some of the most profound experiences, that can only be accessed through language. Such experiences will always be greater than the language with which we describe them, but our words are the symbols that lead to these realities, doorways that provide access to untold experiences. I delight myself in the beauty of words and in the beauty they reveal that lies beyond words.

This journey will include both dangerous terrain and tranquil valleys, both complex arguments and rewarding conclusions. *Simplicity* is such a reward, often only enjoyed after the journey through complexity. Complexity has a beauty and a reward all its own as well. The elegance of true simplicity is supported by depth of understanding. Meaningful simplicity is the summary of complexity; it's the end result of deep and often difficult thought processes. The peaceful lodge at which one arrives at the end of a hard day's hike, filled with food and comfort, is similar to the satisfying simplicity one arrives at after the hard work of navigating the intricate connections of complex ideas. For the mentally lazy there is no simplicity nor mystery, there is only shallowness and certainty... a certainty that is sure to disappoint. How many arm-chair philosophers and theologians have I not encountered, who seem to be content to theorize and carry on about realities they have never experienced, absolutely certain of the logic of their arguments yet blind to the beauty that invites them into an intimacy beyond their theories.

Beauty awakens desire.

We recognize beauty for it somehow finds reflection in us. It disrupts our indifference and draws us to what is worth pursuing. It opens us up to new possibilities as it dissolves the borders between *self* and *other*. We cannot analyze, categorize and shelve beauty together with all the other topics that interest us, for beauty will not be contained. The more we attempt to analyze it, the more we discover about ourselves. The more we interpret it, the more we recognize ourselves. The more we try to ignore it, the more we lose ourselves and our reason for being. Beauty cannot be mastered but unreservedly offers itself in friendship; it can never be controlled but continually invites us to participate in its own reality. This beauty does not subject itself to any one concept or any form of control, nevertheless it reveals itself unexpectedly and gives itself continuously to all who are ready to be astonished. It is this moment of breathless surprise that most accurately describes beauty.

How does one define the infinite?

How can one describe a beauty that extends beyond language? Language finds its greatest fulfillment in symbolizing this beauty and its greatest perversion in claiming to possess it. How difficult it is for words to accurately represent this beauty without pretending to have captured it. Especially because, as one starts to recognize this beauty through language, it is easy to fall in love with the words and never encounter the substance. Yes, language has limits; it cannot capture or reproduce experience, but it can prepare us and introduce us to the reality beyond words.

The concepts and beliefs we have today did not magically appear. They all have histories... surprising histories. Understanding how these ideas were shaped and what contributed to their development are essential if we want to draw maximum benefit from them. Unfortunately, many of these invented concepts have become unconscious assumptions.

To know the origin, development and implications of these ideas is essential if we want to participate in molding them further. We are therefore going to touch on some of the most significant concepts and beliefs that have shaped human history. What does it mean to be human? How is consciousness formed? What gave us a sense of the sacred and how have our ideas of God developed? What is evil and where did the idea of Satan come from? Is time heading anywhere and does our history have a meaningful end? What is the underlying thread that makes all the questions meaningful? In the process of unpacking these questions a whole new environment will be created in which to understand the person of Jesus beyond the religious context in which he is often veiled.

As we distance ourselves from the detail of any one topic and view the connections between these multiple topics, a pattern begins to appear. T.S. Eliot once wrote that the detail of the pattern is movement. And it was Einstein that said: "*Nothing happens until something moves.*" What I intend to show is that the movements within the pattern of these great ideas, are the movements of desire.

2 - MORE THAN MYSELF

I am a wind that cannot be confined
a symbol of a symbol
of a presence,
a breeze,
a movement undefined.

How do I, of myself, get hold...
unless I divide

One to be held   *and one to hold*
One to be found   *and one to hide*

But then, I am not wholly known or held,
for the I that is known, knows nought,
and the I that knows, is a storm unknown.

I am you, this tempest pretends,
concealing its thunder in knowledge, in sense.
Disguising its gales in language,
as it defines and confines
the I that is known, it remains savage.
Never itself does it bow to these rules
or become subject to its own tools.
Assuring us all is calm and all is real,
yet its own substance, it does not reveal.

Can the knower ever be known?
Can the I that is known awake
and see the I that knows?
If possible, I can be whole,
fully known.

I'm beginning to see how blind I've been.
I am much more than the self I've seen.

The undefined can no longer hide.
Reveal yourself! Thunder! Whisper. Abide.
So that I may know,
the one who knows
and together we'll be
I am without boundary.

There is a part of me that pretends to know me. I've come to suspect that this part of me is rather biased and remains hidden behind this pretense of knowledge. As human beings, we are very proficient at telling ourselves stories that secure and comfort our sense of identity. We tend to process all new information in such a way that it confirms what we already believe about ourselves.

But is there maybe more to you than what you are aware of?

What is this *self* you are conscious of?

In this chapter we'll consider the formation of *self* and discover that the *self* you are conscious of is only a small part of what you truly are. Self-consciousness is a deliberate limitation we impose upon ourselves, to protect us from being overwhelmed by what we really are. But consciousness can be expanded to take us beyond the little self we have been so occupied with and bring us into an awareness of something... someone much larger.

The idea that I am an autonomous independent self is attractive for a number of reasons. To view oneself as a separate self-contained entity seems to be the foundation for a sense of identity and individual value. It creates the illusion that I need no one and nothing to be myself. However, neurologists and psychologists tell us that most of what we think, feel, desire and believe has its origin in unconscious processes. We are, for the most part, blissfully unaware of the influences that shape us.

The reality is that we are not independent autonomous beings. We did not come into existence by ourselves, neither do we continue to exist as isolated self-contained creatures. Human beings are completely dependent on the intimate relationships of others to give them existence. The self we become conscious of does not preexist the relationship of our parents. The self is brought into being by relationship and continues to be formed by relational movements. These movements began before conscious awareness and continue largely outside of our awareness.

This brings me to the conclusion that I am more than a self-contained detached entity.

I am found in a web of relationships, a node within a network created by interactions with others and my world. I am formed in a flow of desires and intentions, inseparably woven into this world.

My story is part of a much larger story and despite feelings of autonomy and ideals of individual freedom, I am not myself by myself.

I am more than myself.

I am a reflection... and a reflection needs a reference beyond itself to be whole.

But what energizes these relational movements? Why are we drawn to others like us? Why do children have any interest in their parents? Why do we gravitate towards one another?

No one, to my knowledge, has ever thought of naming the force that draws the child into reproducing what an adult says or does, this force of attraction, interest and attention ... so much of it taken for granted, so much of it a part of the fabric of humanity. A young child has no power to resist that attraction. To feel such attraction is the child's very nature, to the degree that he or she is "normal". A child lacking this capacity would be deprived of something basic to his humanity; he would become isolated, autistic. That natural force of cohesion, which alone grants access to the social, to language, to culture, and indeed to humanness itself, is simultaneously mysterious and obvious, hidden in and of itself, but dazzling in its effects - like gravity and the attraction of corporeal masses in Newtonian space. If gravity did not exist, life on earth would be impossible. Without it, there would be chaos. Similarly, if the remarkable force that attracts human beings to one another, that unites them, that enables children to model themselves on adults, that makes possible their full ontogenesis[1] and, as I just said, their acquisition of language - if this force did not exist, there would be no mankind.[2]

---

1   The development of an individual organism or anatomical or behavioral feature from the earliest stage to maturity.

2   The Puppet of Desire, Jean-Michel Oughourlian, Page 2

I will refer to this force that makes us uniquely human, this capacity for relationship, as mimesis. Mimesis is the process of reflection, the means by which we unconsciously perceive and imitate the intentions or desires of others. It is already present at the very moment in which the self begins to form, as the force that makes consciousness possible. As such it is so pervasive that it is easily overlooked, so present that we take it for granted.

Mirror, mirror, in my brain

The discovery of mirror neurons has given new insight into how this imitative process works. Mirror neurons were first discovered in monkeys, but later research in humans revealed a more complex mirror system.

Mirror neurons operate as follows: When you perform an act such as reaching for an apple and taking a bite, certain neurons become active. Experiments have proven that when you observe this action being performed by another person, many of the same neurons fire as if you were performing the act yourself.

These mirror neurons do not activate with just any observed behavior but only when observing actions that have intent, or observing emotions. Our mimetic ability (our ability to imitate) reaches far deeper than observed actions to the intentions and emotions behind the actions. For the purpose of this discussion, 'intention' and 'desire' can be used interchangeably.

To illustrate: In another research environment, when young children observed a failed attempt to dissemble a toy, it did not deter them from trying alternative methods of accomplishing the same goal. They would often avoid mimicking the failed attempt but would mimic the intention with alternative methods. This demonstrates that humans imitate much more than behavior. We imitate intent and desire. How is this possible? How does one enter the mind of another to know their desires? The discovery of the mirror system gives a neurological basis for understanding mimesis.

IMITATION & AUTHENTICITY.

Imitation often carries negative connotations. Creativity and authenticity seem to imply a kind of genius that needs no model. In our individualistic pursuit of being original, we have therefore resisted the influence of others and sought this originality within ourselves. However, you are not your own originator! Authenticity and originality are therefore not found in your individual self.

I intend to show, paradoxically, that it is our connectedness and ability to imitate that make us uniquely human. You are unique, not as an independent self but rather, you are unique in relationship. There is indeed a special kind of relationship, one that can be called inspirational, which is the source of our authenticity. But let's first look at the connection between imitation and authenticity.

Imitation was a repulsive concept for me from an early age. I enjoyed art and even went to an art school for a period where I studied the great artists. These masters of art each had a style uniquely their own... or so I thought. Some of the greatest artists, like Leonardo da Vinci, openly spoke against imitation.[3]

In this context, imitation became the very opposite of creativity and authenticity.

"*I don't want to imitate, I want to be authentic!*", I thought to myself while studying with great interest the styles and techniques of the masters. The artists I enjoyed most were those whose brush strokes seemed bold and spontaneous. They were obviously comfortable with their own style; it seemed as if they painted without hesitation, drawing from an unrestrained source within them.

I practiced this kind of spontaneous painting. With each repetition my technique improved and eventually I produced a painting with which I was pleased. It was an

---

3   Ackerman, Origins, Imitation, Conventions, 132

No one should ever imitate the maniera of another because he will be called a nephew and not a child of nature with regard to art. Because things in nature exist in such abundance, we need and we ought rather to have recourse to nature than to those masters who have learned from her"

oil painting, produced within a few hours, with bold brush strokes and vibrant colors.

It gave me such a sense of satisfaction because it felt as if I was true to myself. I painted without hesitation, drawing from a boldness within. There was a sense of an undiscovered self being released. The very formation of this self was dependent on claiming these artistic talents and expressions as originating in myself. I was blissfully unaware that what I adored as being an authentic expression of my artistic self was all suggested to me by the art and artists I scrutinized in my studies.

I did not recognize that my desire to imitate no one, was itself an imitation of Da Vinci's desire to imitate no one. Da Vinci himself might not have been aware of the fact that everything he learned, from the language he spoke to the social interactions he had with others, was all learned through a process of imitation.

From an artist's point of view (such as Da Vinci's), it is understandable that explicit imitation would be discouraged. If the very mechanism by which art is produced was exposed, the very qualities that we so adore - the authenticity, originality and genius of the artist - would be threatened. However, creativity is not the complete absence of imitation but rather the unique combination of reflections. The painting I produced was unique, not because nobody influenced me but because of the unique combination of influences and interpretations of those influences.

It is for the same reason that we consciously or unconsciously deny that much of who we are is a reflection of an 'other'. Our very sense of self is dependent on claiming our beliefs and desires as originating in, and belonging to, ourselves. What would happen if we realized that self did not produce our desires, but desires formed self?

This aversion to imitation was not only promoted in art but also in philosophy. The Philosopher René Descartes is probably best known for his statement: "*I think, therefore I am*". His ideas became fundamental in the enlightenment revolution, especially his ideas about the autonomous self which continues to influence our societies to this day.

For Descartes every individual has within himself all that is necessary to judge what is absolute truth, without any reference to any other source or revelation. Within ourselves we are capable of deciding what we desire, what we believe and who we are, without reliance upon anyone or anything else.

In Descartes' view, you are essentially what you think... not what you feel, nor how you behave. And you have within yourself all that is necessary to determine your own thoughts and therefore your own true self.

With the support of such important voices our egos have been assured that we need no one and nothing else but self to be complete. However, there have always been voices who recognized the importance of our ability to imitate. Aristotle said: "*Imitation is natural to man from childhood, one of his advantages over lower animals being this, that he is the most imitative creature in the world, and learns at first by imitation.*"[4]

There have been many voices that have disproved the theory of an individual autonomous self. In the past thirty years many studies have been done on imitation in different branches of science. A good overview can be found in the book "Mimesis and Science".

What they have found concerning imitation is fascinating:

Far from being the simple and mindless act we typically associate with "monkey see, monkey do", imitation is now understood as a complex, generative, and multidimensional phenomenon at the heart of what makes us human. In fact, imitation may very well be the basis for not only how we learn, but also how we understand each other's intentions and desires, establish relational bonds, fall in love, become jealous, compete with one another, and violently destroy

4   The Basic Works of Aristotle, Richard Mckeon

each other, all the while operating largely outside of our conscious awareness.[5]

LIKENESS, OTHERNESS AND SELF

Although there is much research into this area, it doesn't really need a scientific experiment to make plain how essential imitation is.

How does a baby learn to say "Mama" or "Papa"?
We simply repeat the word enough times for the child to mimic us. Typically we will get the child's attention and then say the word.

Imitation begins at a very early age. In fact, studies done by Meltzoff and Moore confirm that newborn babies imitate facial expressions.[6] How does a newborn know that the weird protruding object in front of them equals the mouth on their own face? Before infants have seen their own faces in a mirror, they are able to instinctively map their own faces onto other human beings.

Infants soon begin to recognize when they are being imitated as well, and by 14 months they specifically test whether they are being imitated. This is a way of testing whether they are dealing with another person, someone like themselves. A baby begins life in a type of paradise where there is only the mother and himself/herself. They

---

5   Mimesis and Science, (Location 191) Kindle Edition
6   Meltzoff & Moore, 1997

only have eyes for one another. It is in the context of this gaze that the self begins to form, not as an isolated self but a self that only finds definition in relationship with another. From our earliest moments of life, we become aware of 'others' who are 'like' us. This distinction creates a space for relationship.

A newborn human is one of the most helpless creatures there is. From the moment of birth, humans cry out to others to give them existence. Who we are is bound up in relationship with others. The sense of identity, the consciousness of self, is formed in these interactions with others who are like us. The child begins to differentiate between self and *other* to form a more stable sense of self. This differentiation, however, would not be possible without the *other*. Much of what self is, is owed to others.

We don't reason ourselves into consciousness. There are more fundamental forces at play. Neurologists have suggested three stages and categories of self awareness: "*the protoself and its primordial feelings; the action-driven core self; and finally the autobiographical self, which incorporates social and spiritual dimensions.*"[7] What is of importance to our discussion is that the first and most fundamental part of self-formation is not *reason* but *feeling*, after which follows action and our own personal histories. A baby does

---

7   Damasio, Antonio (2010-11-09). Self Comes to Mind: Constructing the Conscious Brain (Kindle Locations 256-257). Knopf Doubleday Publishing Group. Kindle Edition.

not follow a logical argument to determine whether he or she is hungry - he/she simply feels hungry. Consciousness begins as a feeling beyond reason. Reason develops as we attempt to describe these feelings and the actions that flow from them. The most fundamental self is found in this place of awareness - an awareness without history, without any reference beyond the moment. It is only after this moment of consciousness that the autobiographical self, the self that claims memories as belonging to itself, begins to develop. This primordial feeling needs clearer definition for us to better understand our formation. Mimesis - our reflective nature - gives much needed insight into this process. What will be shown is that the self-of-feeling, the self-of-action and the autobiographical self can all be summarized as the self-of-desire.

The process by which we understand others and find ourselves in relationship with others, is mimesis. We imitate intentions, desires, emotions and actions... and we do it largely unconsciously. Possibly, mimesis needs to be unconscious in order for the sense of self to form.

> ... researchers also note how difficult it is for most people to believe that they are imitating and being influenced by others in such broad and automatic ways, even when they are presented with evidence that indicates otherwise. The tendency to deny our own imitative behavior may be due to its non conscious operation, combined with the fact that

such knowledge threatens the notion of our selves as being primary conscious and in control ...[8]

SELF AND DESIRE.

We saw how self is formed in relationship with others, as a differentiation takes place between self and others like self. Both likeness and otherness are required for self to form. Likeness suggests the possibility of connection; otherness creates the space necessary for relational movement. We will now get more specific and look at the interaction of self and desire.

We noticed how a newborn typically begins life in a type of paradise where there is only the mother and himself/herself. They only have eyes for one another. But soon the baby notices that the mother looks elsewhere as well. Human eyes, with their large white spaces, make it particularly easy to follow eye movements. The baby soon becomes interested in what interests the mother.

Imitating these eye movements is the beginning of lifelong suggestions as to what is desirable. Human capacity to imitate the desires of others is by far the most significant aspect of imitation and the most unconscious. In other words, desire does not flow directly between self and an object, but rather - desire is mediated.

---

8   Mimesis and Science, (Kindle Location 758) Kindle Edition

Experiments to show the importance of a gaze to communicate desire have been done with children between the ages of one and one and a half.[9] The child would be placed opposite the adult. The adult would turn their head with open eyes and gaze at an object. The experiment was repeated with a number of children. The majority of children would follow the adult's gaze. However, when the same experiment was done with the adult closing their eyes before turning their head, a majority of children no longer mimicked the head movement. The gaze of another person somehow gave the object value and so made it of interest to the child. From the earliest age, the gaze of others suggests what is desirable.

In a situation of conflict, where two children compete for the same object, it is not uncommon to hear the argument: "I saw it first" or "I wanted it first". The child does not know that it was probably the gaze of another that suggested the desirability of the object. The illusion that the desire originated in an 'I' is essential to establish a sense of self. Claiming these desires as our own is part of the process of differentiating ourselves from others; it is the birth of the self-of-desire. The very origin of this self is therefore one of fundamental ignorance or even deception for in claiming these desires as originating in and belonging to self, we do not recognize the process by which they were suggested to

9   Rechele Brooks and Andrew Meltzoff. "The importance of eyes" Developmental Psychology.

us. The further formation of this self will continue in this fundamental error of claiming ownership and perceiving itself as the origin of its beliefs and wants. As we mature we enter a sphere where desires are communicated to us by a variety of ways, not only by those closest to us but also by the cultures and communities we find ourselves in. In order to maintain a stable sense of self, we continue in the conviction that *self* is the originator of our desires... not realizing that desire is suggested to us by another. Of all the qualities that we reflect, desire is the quality whose movements are most elusive.

Mimetic desire has huge implications, for it means that desire is not produced individually but rather has its origin in relationship. Desire constantly moves in the spaces between us, and by its very movement, carves and energizes our characters. Desire is not created by self, but rather self is formed by desire. That means that you are not the sole source of your desires but rather you have your origin in the desires that formed you. Self is therefore not an independent substance or reality that exists by itself, rather, it is a self-of-desire. Self is constantly deconstructed and reconstructed - a dynamic construct that is deeply dependent on realities beyond itself. As such I need a reference beyond myself to know myself.

In this chapter we explored the question: Who or what are you? It is in replacing this question with three more revealing questions that we come closer to an answer.

Firstly, what do you desire?
Desire is a very subtle movement... so elusive that we most often do not detect its coming until it is present, pretending to originate in *self*. Desire is the movement that animates us.

Secondly, where does this desire come from?
Once we acknowledge that desire does not spontaneously arise within ourselves, or between ourselves and the object of desire, we will be much more perceptive regarding its origin. Desires are mediated.

Lastly, does *self* create desire, or does desire form *self*?
This might be a challenge to the very concept of what you thought you were, but it might also open up possibilities of being, you never knew of before.

3 - DESIRE FOUND ME

The Genesis narrative is filled with mimetic symbolism. Likeness and otherness, God and man, male and female, differentiation, desire, paradise, romance, whispering voices and the confusion of good and evil are all present in the first three chapters. We are about to unfold Genesis 1 to 3 within this mimetic context, exploring both the life-giving and destructive possibilities of our reflective nature. The historic, cultural and literary context of the Genesis narrative will be discussed in greater depth in chapter 6.

Desire can be the most life-giving force, inspiring us to give ourselves completely to another; it can also be a most destructive force, causing us to harm others and ourselves. How does one distinguish between life-giving and destructive desire?

CREATING DIFFERENCES

Reflective desire needs an environment in which to function, a space in which to flow. Difference or distinction is what makes this space available. Where there is no difference there is only formless chaos - boring sameness. Difference establishes a creative distance, a space that makes relationship possible. However, difference can be perceived as contradiction and consequently, distance then becomes a space for conflict. So, difference can be perceived either as a threatening contradiction or as an opportunity for reconciliation. Reconciliation, in this context, is not the reduction of all differences to sameness but rather the continual moving towards, a drawing closer, in which differences are maintained in a playful harmony.

How to make sense of the connections between seeming opposites has always been the quest of spiritual and philosophical thought. How can contradictions be anything but meaningless chaos? Can we find a common source in which light and darkness co-exist?

In the beginning God created the heaven and the earth. And the earth was without form, and void; and darkness was upon the face of the deep. And the Spirit of God moved upon the face of the waters.
(Genesis 1:1–2 KJV)

In the beginning of God's preparing the heavens and the earth — the earth hath existed waste and void, and darkness [is] on the face of the deep, and the Spirit of God fluttering on the face of the waters
(Genesis 1:1–2 YNG)

God begins creating by ordering the chaos, bringing form to the formless, by increasing differentiation and assigning functions. First he separates light from darkness and day from night. Then he separates the waters above from the waters below. On day three, he separates the waters below from dry land. Creation is a process of bringing into being meaningful differences, of giving distinct form.

The first three days are concerned with creating different spaces, while the next three periods are concerned with filling these spaces and assigning functions. Accordingly, day one corresponds to day four, day two to five and three to six.

On day one God separated the light from the darkness and the day from night. On day four he fills these spaces by creating the sun to rule the day and the lesser luminaries, the stars and the moon, to rule the night. On day five he fills the spaces created on day two with fish and sea creatures filling the waters, and fowl filling the sky. All that remains to be populated is the dry land - earth. Day six is used to create land animals and man.

The way in which God creates is also very co-operative. He doesn't create fish by himself in a heavenly aquarium and then throw them into the sea. No! He calls on the waters to participate in this creative act and to bring forth the sea creatures. "*Let the waters bring forth...*"[1] He calls on the earth to produce the animals. God is the source of creation and calls on creation to be part of the creative process. This is not a picture of an external God acting upon a separate creation, but rather of a God intimately involved in every natural process. This God is no demiurge - a separate entity that exists independently from creation - but rather he is the source of all existence, the reason why there is something rather than nothing. Creation is therefore not a singular event that happened a long time ago but rather every moment is an act of creation and existence itself is evidence that our Creator is closer than we imagined. Yet despite this intimate connection there remains an infinite difference. God distinguishes what is not himself and in this act of distinction, this gift of distance, creation happens.

This process of differentiation, separation and ordering is further emphasized by living creatures being categorized into different species. Interestingly, the word species in Latin comes from the same root word as *speculum*, which means 'mirror'. A species is a group of individuals that mirror one another more accurately than those outside the group.

Mankind is created last, in a species of its own - a being designed to mirror God.

---

1   Genesis 1:20

IMAGE & LIKENESS

And God said, Let us make man in our image, after our likeness (Genesis 1:26 KJV).

The very definition of man is a being that reflects, one that does not exist in isolation but in a relation of likeness.[2] In other words, you cannot be yourself by yourself. Humanity has been given the unique capability to be whatever it beholds.

It is also significant that the word God (Elohim), used in Genesis 1:1, is in the plural form. Again in verse 26, God is referred to as "us". God, according to this narrative, is not an isolated singularity but a communion, a relationship. Difference is at the very core of what God is. Difference is what makes fellowship possible. Difference creates a space in which desire can flow. God's oneness does not consist in formless sameness but in holding all the differences together. In other words, God is not one-and-the-same, but one-and-distinct.

---

2   Likeness

The verb is also an ideal one for the author of the Song of Solomon where the respective lovers search for appropriate figures of speech to convey their depth of love for each other: Song 2:9, 17; 7:8; 8:14; 1:9 (Piel).
In the Piel stem the verb assumes the meaning "to compare, imagine, think, intend."
The word "likeness" rather than diminishing the word "image" actually amplifies it and specifies its meaning. Man is not just an image but a likeness-image. He is not simply representative but representational. Man is the visible, corporeal representative of the invisible, bodiless God. תומד guarantees that man is an adequate and faithful representative of God on earth (Clines).
"ד מ ה," TWOT, n.p.

Humanity is said to be created in a relationship of likeness to this community. Humanity's very essence is relationship. We are to image, to imitate, the very relationship that is God. The God in whom all distinctions have their source and continue to exist in harmony rather than contradiction, has extended himself in a creature capable of doing the same - one capable of seeing the beauty in the contrasts.

The scene is set. All that is necessary for reflection, for mimesis, is in place. There is *likeness* and *otherness*, differentiation that allows a sense of self to form in relation to an *other* that is *like* me. Only one thing is missing: the initiating desire, the movement that will bridge the distance between self and other. What desire will define man? What event will suggest to man what is valuable and what is worth pursuing? What act will begin mimetic movement?

And God blessed them...
(Genesis 1:28 KJV)

God recognizes the beauty of his image and likeness in man. He desires and loves this distinct expression of himself and takes the initiative to demonstrate his love. 'Barak', the word we have translated as 'blessed', carries the meaning of an act of adoration. God's adoration is the initiating desire. This act of 'barak', of adoration, is the breath of life, the wind that blew over chaos, the spirit that communicates the desire of God.

God is the *other* that animates and pervades the *self*. Without this other, the self will have no breath, no movement, no life. He is the part that makes me more than an isolated self but a mysterious self in constant flux, intermingled with the otherness of God.

Man's first and formative conscious experience, according to this Genesis account, is of God's adoration, God's blessing, God's self-giving love. To absorb and reflect this love is to participate in this relationship of likeness. Humanity is all God imagines her to be as she beholds the One who adores her, allowing this adoration to define her as she reflects it back. "*We love, because He first loved us*" (1 John 4:19).

This is a vision of ideal reflection, ideal mimesis. God's desire for me awakens my desire for him. His relentless pursuit of me sustains my passion for him. I have found my true reflection. In this place of mutual exchange there is no rivalry. This 'likeness' does not create the desire to replace the other but to partake of the other. Intimacy rather than rivalry is the result. Even God's otherness does not frighten me but entices me to explore.

Desire found me
formed me,
scattered thoughts, collected,
Over formless confusion, whispered.

From where, this desire comes?
From I! It is mine ... I thought.
I made it, from I it came forth.
All the while, I was my desire's form.
To desire I belong.

Empty intentions you did fill,
this heart, with affection, you caused to spill,
loved your life into human form,
in your passion I was born.
Dreamt of me,
that I may be.

Love reflected meets love initiated as man and God meet face to face. Only here am I whole for here I am more than myself; I am a reflection of God. This is union. I am truly more than an individual self.

Union implies more than one part coming together. Union is not one-and-the-same but rather one-and-distinct. Reflection implies more than one entity, namely, that which is reflected and that which reflects.

In other words, as a creature who reflects, there needs to be another besides myself to complete who I am. In this context the *other* becomes an integral part of *self*. There is otherness in me and part of me is in another. And the space between is not empty or stagnant but consists of a continual flow, an inexhaustible partaking of one another - the highest form of mimetic desire.

A NEW DIFFERENCE

In the second creation account (Genesis 2:5-24) another important difference is created. Two trees are identified: the tree of life, and the tree of the knowledge of good and evil. This is the difference between that which is life-giving and that which is death-producing. The tree of the knowledge of good and evil comes with a clear warning: "*you shall not eat, for in the day that you eat of it you shall surely die.*" This also identifies mankind's most primordial fear, the fear of death as a form of punishment.

The very presence of the tree represents the possibility of evil and the liberty of man to oppose the Divine will. The tree does not bear different fruits, some good and some evil. No, it bears one fruit in which the knowledge of good and evil are mixed together. It speaks of a fusion... or a *confusion* between good and evil.

Another difference is created as God separates male and female.

Then the LORD God said, "It is not good for the man to be alone. I will make a helper as his complement. (Genesis 2:18 HCSB)

The word we translated 'complement' can also be translated 'opposite'. Again, both otherness and likeness need to be present for love to be fulfilled.

God presents this gift to Adam, thereby suggesting Eve's value and desirability. Adam is delighted as he recognizes both likeness and difference (otherness) in her. Desire awakens desire, love awakens love. The mimetic cycle, originally ignited by God, continues to energize this relationship as Adam's desire for Eve breathes life into their relationship. The human capacity to reflect finds fulfillment within this relationship.

NAKEDNESS

In Genesis 2:25 we read: "*Both the man and his wife were naked (arum), yet felt no shame.*" In the next verse we read: "*Now the serpent was more subtle (arum) than any beast of the field*". So we translated "*arum*" as *naked* in one instance and as *subtle* in another - why?

Genesis 42:9 might help to explain. Here Joseph says: "*You are spies! You have come to see the nakedness of the land!*" The accusation is that they have come to find the places where the borders are vulnerable to penetration.

To be naked is to be vulnerable. This condition has the potential for either intimacy or harm. *"The man and his wife were both naked, yet felt no shame."* They felt no shame because they had never used this condition of vulnerability to harm each another. The serpent is more 'arum' than any of the other beasts. Unlike most other creatures the serpent has no hands and no feet with which to protect itself. As such, the serpent is an ideal symbol of this vulnerability and how it can be twisted to harm.

SERPENT OF TWISTED MIMETIC DESIRE

We have everything needed for a very exciting story: A naked girl and guy, magical trees, talking animals, a luscious garden full of desirable fruit...! The writers, however, had much more in mind than a historic romantic novel. They were unveiling a process that is as relevant to us today, as it ever was to any prehistoric humans we can imagine.

Now the serpent was more subtle than any beast of the field which the LORD God had made. And he said unto the woman, Yea, hath God said, Ye shall not eat of every tree of the garden? And the woman said unto the serpent, We may eat of the fruit of the trees of the garden: But of the fruit of the tree which is in the midst of the garden, God hath said, Ye shall not eat of it, neither shall ye touch it, lest ye die. And the serpent said unto the woman, Ye shall not surely die: For God doth know that in the day ye eat thereof, then your eyes shall be opened, and ye shall be as gods, knowing good and evil. And when the woman saw that the tree was good for food, and that it was pleasant to the eyes, and a tree to be desired to make one wise, she took of the fruit thereof, and did eat, and gave also unto her husband with her; and he did eat. And the eyes of them both were opened, and they knew that they were naked; and they sewed fig leaves together, and made themselves aprons. (Genesis 3:1–7 KJV)

If reflected (mimetic) desire is what makes the greatest good and the greatest evil possible, then these ancient intuitions of the writers of Genesis 3, describing the mixture of good and evil, are very apt indeed.

The first prohibition man became aware of had to do with the curbing of appetite, the limitation of desire. The words and phrases used in this story point so clearly to desire and the consequences of desire perverted: eat, fruit, touch, eyes, ye shall be as gods, knowing good and evil, saw that the tree was good, pleasant to the eyes, desired to make one wise, naked. Ironically, it is always the very law that prohibits, that stirs desire for that prohibition.

Notice how desire is mediated. The woman only sees the tree and its fruit as desirable after it is suggested to her. A very different perception of God, compared to Genesis 1, is proposed here. The suggestion is made that God does not want man to be like him and therefore has prohibited man from eating from this tree. It implies that God desires this tree more than any other tree and therefore withholds it from mankind. Simultaneously it implies that man lacks being. The *likeness* that is on offer here is a perverted likeness - one that is in competition with God and attempts to replace God. In a brilliant twist by the serpent, God's desire is placed in opposition to man's desire. God's desire for the tree is portrayed and perceived as rivalry, for he withholds from man what he desires for himself.

In the first creation account (Genesis 1), man is created in God's image and likeness. In that context, reflected desire is beautiful and makes intimacy possible. Man is like God without being in competition with God. Unlike the pure mimetic desire of Genesis 1 where man reflects the God who gives his own likeness to man, here in Genesis 3 a third object of desire is introduced. The suggestion is made that God withholds this object from man, which in turn implies that man is lacking something. The lack suggested, however, is not simply the fruit of the tree but rather the likeness of God. The nature of this lack is therefore not simply a lack of possession, but a lack of being - a sense of insufficiency.

Misinterpreting God's desire awakens equivalently perverse desires in man. For if man perceives that God desires this tree more than any other, but withholds it from man, then this tree becomes more desirable than any other tree. The moment that man perceives God as a rival that withholds, is the moment in which mimetic desire is twisted from a life-giving source to a lack-conscious, death-producing force. We reflect the God we perceive. Adoration becomes accusation and trust is replaced with suspicion. The desire to partake of God is twisted into a desire to replace God and so the true self that is intermingled with the otherness of God is substituted with an independent self. We alienate ourselves from God and we alienate this newly created self from our true selves. Twisted desire perverts and makes us incomprehensible to ourselves. Our misunderstanding of God's intention becomes the reflection we project onto God. Direct communion with God is thereby replaced by a mediated relationship with our projections. To distinguish between the real God and our projections becomes virtually impossible.

SERPENT SYMBOLISM

In later chapters we will look at the origin of myth and also how the scriptures relate to myth. Many of these early stories were concerned with the origin of the cosmos and man, and the battles between good and evil. We will look at both similarities and differences between myth and scripture in chapter 6. At this stage I only want to draw your attention to one important difference. Almost all origin myths from this period perceived evil as a reality older than creation itself. In these stories the gods had personal histories full of conflict in a dimension before and beyond our world. The chaos, the formless and the meaningless, are always already there and it is only through creative violence that the world of mankind came into being.

When the Genesis creation account does away with all the prehistory of the gods - with the very existence of such gods - it also makes a very definite statement about evil. Evil does not preexist the goodness of God's creation. It has no eternal other-worldly origin. The clear and shocking declaration of Genesis 3 is that evil has a human origin. The same insight would later be repeated by James:

> *Let no one say when he is tempted, "I am being tempted by God," for God cannot be tempted with evil, and he himself tempts no one. But each person is tempted when he is lured and enticed by his own desire. Then desire when it has conceived gives birth to sin, and sin when it is fully grown brings forth death.*
> (James 1:13–15 ESV)

The only mythical creature that does survive this Genesis 3 retelling of human origins is the serpent. Even then, the text makes it clear that the serpent too, is a creature made by God. If evil does have a purely human origin, why retain the serpent symbol? As we have seen above, the serpent represents the psychological projection of human desire. Desire is a process that reaches both within and without us.

It is a part within us that we do not recognize and therefore, continually externalize. As such the serpent is a perfect metaphor for the twisted cycle of perverted mimetic desire.

However, if evil was only portrayed as an internal human process, then the only conclusion possible would be that mankind is inherently evil. But God's declaration that man is very good obviously contradicts such a conclusion. Evil as a possibility, a process in which we need to participate before it becomes concrete reality, both justifies God as the creator of good and keeps mankind responsible for our world. The serpent as external symbol of the possibility of evil, means that man is not internally utterly depraved by nature. Every person discovers evil as a process already present in their world. Whether we participate in it or not, is every person's choice.

The very condition - mimetic desire - that made intimacy possible, also made mankind vulnerable. It is only after partaking of this fruit that we become ashamed of our vulnerability, that is, of our ability to be harmed and to harm. So begins the process of making ourselves clothing, protective layers that will keep us from being harmed... but at the same time keep us from the intimacy we were designed for.

And the LORD God said, Behold, the man is become as one of us, to know good and evil.

(Genesis 3:22 KJV)

Regarding this verse, the French Philosopher Paul Ricoeur writes:

> *...the serpent has not spoken altogether falsely; the era opened up to freedom through fault is a certain experience of infinity that hides from us the finite situation of the creature, the ethical finiteness of man. Henceforth the evil infinite of human desire - always something else, always something more - which animates the movements of civilizations, the appetite for pleasure, for possessions, for power, for knowledge - seems to constitute the reality of man. The restlessness that makes us discontented with the present seems to be our true nature, or rather the absence of nature that makes us free. In a way the promise of the serpent marks the birth of a human history drawn by its idols towards the infinite...*[3]

In this sense man did indeed become like God, but it is a very different likeness than what was spoken of in Genesis 1:26 In the first account, likeness is a gift from God that enables relationship, enables a mutual partaking of one another without rivalry. In the second account, likeness is presented as a position of equality that we lack which in turn stirs our desire to acquire it, even if it means rivalry with God. The desire that unites in the first becomes a

---

3   Paul Ricoeur, The Symbolism of Evil, Page 254

desire that divides in the second. The latter is a likeness we pursue in rivalry with God - a God we perceive as withholding this likeness. Man's opposition to the love and life of God would indeed become a rivalry that would give birth to much pain, suffering and death throughout human history.

This mixture of good and evil confused our conceptions of God, of ourselves, of our world. Twisted desire is what gave birth to perversion. It is this harmful perversion that I refer to as sin. Sin placed God and our true selves beyond the grasp of our understanding. This confusion would be reflected in our history and in the stories we told about our imagined history.

SUMMARY

In chapter 2 we began discovering how intrinsic desire is to who we are. In this chapter, we have continued to explore the environments in which desire thrives. And so we have re-read Genesis 1 to 3 with this model in mind. Difference forms a space in which desire can move. God creates by transforming formless chaos into meaningful differences.

As the crescendo of his self-expression, mankind is created in the image and likeness of God. It is both our likeness to and distinction from God that make intimacy possible. This is the highest form of mimetic desire: a situation in which we partake of one another without entering into rivalry with one another. God gives himself freely to us and we spontaneously and gratefully reflect this love back to him and one another.

However, the environment can also be re-configured in such a way that desire becomes twisted and destructive. The distance created by difference can be perceived as contradiction. Contradiction can awaken fear, and fear distorts our vision. When we step outside the life-giving embrace of the One who made us to be adored, a sense of inadequacy can easily take hold. Such anxiety becomes an ideal environment in which desire can be perverted into a destructive evil. In such an environment, desire becomes fear motivated and rivalistic. A sense of inadequacy energizes our desires to acquire whatever 'fruit' promises to restore to us the likeness of God.

This fundamental blindness sets us on a path of destruction, which is the topic of the next chapter.

Mimetic Desire of Genesis 1	Twisted Mimetic Desire of Genesis 3
1. Two parties: God and man.	A third object of desire: the fruit of the forbidden tree.
2. Self-giving love. he gives his own image and likeness.	Withholding the fruit and consequently keeping mankind from being like him.
3. No sense of lack.	A sense of lack is suggested.
4. Mankind is the recipient of God's image, likeness and adoration.	Mankind takes the fruit and pursues likeness to God.
5. Direct relationship - mimetic reflection.	Projected image of God, subject to interpretation and misunderstanding. We reflect our own projections.

4 - Desiring Your Neighbor's Ass

Mimesis, the human reflective capacity that makes us most like God - able to love - is also the capacity for the greatest evils, namely hatred, conflict and violence. The very quality that makes us more than animals is also the quality that causes men to stoop much lower than animals.

When we lose sight of the God who adores us, when this God is no longer the source of our desires, we simply don't know what we desire and start searching, mostly unaware of our quest. Soon we begin to reflect the confusion and desires of those around us.

Adoration turns to accusation.
Affirmation turns to suspicion.
The very quality that was meant to draw us into intimacy, as we behold and reflect the love of another who is like us, can lead to the greatest isolation when we misinterpret the intentions of the one we unconsciously mimic.

Let me illustrate. Two young boys may become best of friends because of shared interests. Their enjoyment of similar activities, such as fishing and hiking, forges a bond between them. Each may think that these desires originate within himself, that he is individually the origin and owner of his own desires, and that he was simply lucky to find a friend with whom he has so much in common. The fact that their desires are interactive and mutually reinforcing is mostly beyond the conscious level. Mimicking one another's desires provides a basis for a beautiful friendship as they grow into adulthood.

Then it happens!
Both notice the same girl.
Both fall in love.
Both are oblivious to how much their friend has contributed to what they think is their own desire. What was once the basis for friendship, now becomes the reason for conflict. Mimesis sustains their rivalry as much as it once sustained their friendship.

> *Like gravity, mimesis is at once a force of attraction and a force of repulsion: imitation begins as discipleship, in which the model is taken simply as a model. But before long, the imitation of a gesture will cause the model and the disciple to grasp at the same object: the model will become a rival, and mimesis will take on the character of a conflict. In this way mimesis engenders both attraction and repulsion; in this way it produces both discipleship and conflict, nonviolent and violent acquisition, peace and war, alliance*

and tension, fighter and opponent, likeness and difference - or should one say it gives rise to the difference as such? Just as gravity, which hurls bodies against one another, is at the same time the condition of their separation, that is, of their individual existence, so also mimesis, the force of attraction between human beings, assures by their very workings their concrete distinctness, their simultaneous identity and individuality - in a word, their particular existence.[1]

René Girard and Mimetic Theory

We have looked at the human ability to reflect, to mirror. Up to now we have illustrated these concepts on a personal and interpersonal level: Mimesis and desire, desire and the formation of self, unconscious mimesis in personal relationships. As we continue our discoveries of the presence and effect of mimesis in larger groups and communities, I think it is a good time to introduce René Girard and his discovery of mimetic theory.

René is a French historian, literary critic and philosopher of culture. His thoughts have influenced many branches of science including anthropology, theology, psychology, mythology, sociology, literary criticism, economics, cultural studies, and philosophy. In each of these areas there is a growing body of literature that builds on the work of Girard. The fact that so many branches of science

---

1   Jean-Michel Oughourlian, The Puppet of Desire,

have seriously engaged with Girard's mimetic theory is testimony to its broad power of explanation. Mimetic theory, or mimetic realism as some prefer to call it, can be summarized as follows:

1 - Desire is mimetic.
Much has been written and said about desire from the earliest literature. The same is true for mimesis. What René Girard made the world aware of is how these two are connected - desire is suggested by another.

2 - Mimetic rivalry and conflict originate in mimetic desire. When two hands reach for the same object, conflict is most often the result.

3 - In early human groupings, mimetic violence resulted in scapegoating - the single victim mechanism. This represents the birth of sacrifice, which became ritual - the basis of archaic religion and culture.

4 - The Bible reveals all of the above, whereas myth tries to conceal the violence or the innocence of the victim. The Biblical scriptures are unique in making us aware of the scapegoating mechanism and thereby condemning it.

MIMESIS AND HUMAN HISTORY
What do these concepts look like in practice?

Peering into our prehistoric past, attempting to understand the problems our ancestors faced and how they went about solving them, is obviously a very complicated task. There are many studies that focus on particular events, such as the transition from hunter-gatherer societies to agricultural communities. What follows is by no means a comprehensive overview of these processes. Its purpose is to give a specific example of how mimesis could have influenced the development of civilization.

How did early human communities form? Family units obviously provided the most basic structure, but how did small and simple family groups develop into complex social structures?

When primitive groups met, violence often erupted. However, there were obvious benefits of joining forces as well. More effective hunting, diversifying the means and methods of finding food, safety in numbers - these are but a few of the benefits. However, imagine such an early community in which there were no formal laws. Conflict was inevitable. Because desire is mimetic, competition, rivalry and violence would thrive in groups where there were no prohibitions to violence. Unlike most animals, humans do not seem to know at what point to stop rivalry - they will fight until someone dies.

Significantly, human sacrifice seems to be a universal phenomenon and the first sign of a new civilization. Archaeological evidence shows that most of these early communities were religious or at least ritualistic. Some form of sacrificial system was at the heart of primitive communities.[2] Why?

The example I will use is set in the context of an ancient agricultural community. It is important, though, to realize that sacrificial practices were present among hunter-gatherer groups as well. In fact it might well have been the development of rituals that prompted the transition to agricultural communities.

From a scientific standpoint there is no generally accepted model accounting for the origin of agriculture, above all in the consideration that agriculture was anti-economic.

Agriculture, far from being a natural and upward step, in fact led commonly to a lower quality of life. Hunter-gatherers typically do less work for the same amount of food, are healthier, and are less prone to famine than primitive farmers: why was this behaviour (agriculture) reinforced (and hence selected for) if it was not offering adaptational rewards surpassing those accruing to hunter-gathering or foraging economies?[3]

2   Raymond Schwager, Banished From Eden, Page 97
3   Wadley, Martin 1993: 96; also Lee, De Vore 1968, Cohen 1989.

In other words, changing from a hunter-gatherer community to an agricultural settlement was not motivated by a better lifestyle, better health, or more food. So why change?

Girard gives this insight:

> *The hunter-gatherers started to settle permanently because of **the increasing importance of ritual sites** and the complexity of the rituals of which they were part, and which in turn produced, the domestication of animals and the discovery of agriculture. Climate changes or particular soil conditions were also important elements in this later development, but the discovery was very likely to have been made around the sacred burial sites in which any symbolic activity of the primitive community was carried out (such as **burying seeds along with human beings**, for instance).[4]* [Emphasis mine]

What this suggests is that it might well have been the sacred rituals associated with death and burial that provided a key motivation for hunter-gatherer communities to become more settled.

MIMETIC DESIRE AND CONFLICT

The example I will use is purely fictional, however, Girard and others have offered countless examples of text, from ancient myths to accounts from the middle ages, to modern conflicts, that follow the same pattern.

---

4   Girard 2008

Let's imagine an early agricultural community. The desire for a certain commodity, such as goats, will fuel the desire of others to also possess goats. There will be an ever increasing desire to own goats, however, there are only a limited amount of goats. Unlimited desire and limited resources creates an environment primed for conflict.

Being oblivious to the origin of our desires, we claim preeminence for our desires: "*I wanted it first.*" Because desire is mimetic we sense in a very personal way the intention of the other to own the object we want ourselves. The schemes we make to outwit the opposition, mixed with our reflective nature, suggest to us that our rival is making similar schemes. Suspicion begins to scrutinize the opposition for signs that might confirm our fearful imaginations. Confirming signs soon appear.

Rivals often don't know that they are imitating each other. As desire for an object intensifies into rivalry, the object becomes less important and the rival becomes more important. The sense of lack that awakens these desires is not only a sense of lacking the object(goats), but rather a sense of insufficiency - a lack of being. Desire to possess the object, which is an imitation of the rival's desire, grows into a desire to replace the rival. The model of the desire becomes more desirable than the object of desire in this perverted cycle. But the model is a rival and so the only way to satisfy desire is to replace the model. The desire for an object masks the fundamental desire, which is a desire for being. This can escalate into a situation where one no longer only claims the superiority of one's desire, but one claims the superiority of one's existence.

Early law codes, in a variety of civilizations, are all focused on prohibiting or at least controlling violence. Within the ten commandments we can see the mimetic process in inverse order:

> *Thou shalt not kill.*
> *Thou shalt not commit adultery.*
> *Thou shalt not steal.*
> *Thou shalt not bear false witness against thy neighbour.*[5]

It is as if the writer can go on and on about what we "*shalt not*" do and then decides to get to the heart of the matter:

> *Thou shalt not covet thy neighbour's house, thou shalt not covet thy neighbour's wife, nor his manservant, nor his maidservant, nor his ox, nor his ass, nor any thing that is thy neighbour's.*[6]

At the heart of conflict and harmful behavior is a craving, a desire for what belongs to another. Such unfulfilled desire can lead to deceitful dealings ("*bear false witness*"). In early communities where laws were not yet in force, the next

---

5   Exodus 20:13–16 KJV
6   Exodus 20:17 KJV

step would be to simply take what you want ("*thou shalt not steal*"). But remember, at the heart of this conflict is a deep sense of insufficiency; what we really are grasping for is *being*. We don't simply want what our neighbor has, we want to replace the model and so we take what is most dear: "*Thou shalt not commit adultery.*" If this cycle of escalating conflict is not stopped, the final crime is to kill.

(The verse previously quoted was the inspiration for this chapter's title. Most modern translations use the word "donkey" instead, but I still prefer "ass"!)

ESCALATING VIOLENCE

What started as innocent desire develops into competition. Competition in itself is not bad, but if there are no prohibitions against violence competition often spills over into violence. Violence in turn will continue to escalate if allowed to go unchecked. One conflict gives rise to another. One act of violence stirs the fires of revenge. The energy produced by the movement of desire between two people greatly increases within groups, just as the gravitational pull of bodies is directly related to their mass and the distance between them. The proverbial "straw that broke the camel's back", a final event or act that sets in motion the mob, begins a movement of uncontrollable violence. Boundaries become blurred. Violence has little respect for position or status. As differentiation within these communities collapses, so does order.

SCAPEGOATING

It is at the very height of this conflict, at the point where it seems to be a war of all against all and the community is about to disintegrate, that some communities find a way to preserve themselves. The war of all against all is transformed into a war of all against one. A single victim is chosen. In the very act of finding a scapegoat the fragmented and broken community becomes united in their enmity against the minority group or the one. Old enemies are reconciled as they find a common, new enemy.

In the fervor of the moment the selection of the scapegoat is largely spontaneous, but certain criteria seem to apply naturally. The person is normally a bit different: the prettiest (source of jealousy) or the ugliest, a new arrival or a foreigner. The most important criteria, though, is to minimize the potential for retribution. If the victim does not have a large family or friendship circle, it makes the task at hand much easier and minimizes future reprisals.

FOUNDING MURDER

As the community externalizes their own evil and projects it onto the scapegoat the victim is demonized, symbolizing everything that is wrong in the community. Usually the accusations include the kind of crimes that disrupt the natural order such as incest and bestiality. Different offenses, multiple conflicts, melt into one that contains the emotion and frustration of them all. A communal catharsis takes place. The community is unanimous in their verdict. The reason for our conflict, the source of our frustration has been found. Blind rage is not subject to reason, but reason has often been employed by rage to justify its actions. The sacrificial scapegoat is undoubtedly guilty - the community, undoubtedly innocent.

A communal murder happens.
The chaos ceases.
Order is restored.
As if waking from a drunken stupor, the community begins to recognize something truly horrific: the corpse of their victim. The meaning of the moment might be clearer if we imagine ourselves as part of the surviving community. What horror as we begin to realize that we have murdered one of our own, one like us, and we did it intentionally. Faced with the lifeless body of the one we destroyed, there is a sense that something is deeply wrong. The corpse is the most powerful symbol of the absence of being and evokes the dread of losing one's own being, especially in those who participated in the violence. The most basic fear is evoked - the fear of death. We dread facing the same fate. Dread is the greatest of fears for it is the fear of losing one's being. If one, just like me, could suffer such a fate, what prevents me from suffering the same fate. Our nakedness is exposed, our vulnerability becomes a fearful

reality. And if I participated in the violence, the threat of vengeance becomes a foreboding possibility. Whereas dread is the fear of losing one's being, guilt is the sense of unworthiness of being.

This moment in which we recognize the corpse becomes even more sacred as the eerie silence reveals that the violence has stopped. A magical peace has come. The peace and sacred unity that has come to the community stands in complete contrast to a mutilated, lifeless corpse. The greatest blessing and the greatest horror, tangible peace and overwhelming fear are simultaneously present. The victim brings death, but a death that guarantees life for the survivors. The fear of death and the desire for life are present at once. Our sense of the sacred is formed in this moment in which we stand in grateful awe of the peace that has come and in dreadful angst at the sight of our victim. Is this the event in which we begin to partake of the knowledge of good and evil? Is this the moment in our prehistoric past in which we fuse and therefore *confuse* good and evil?

The effect of this founding murder is profound. The community that was torn apart by conflict, at the verge of disintegration, suddenly finds themselves united, at peace and stronger than they have ever been before. The mindless violence that recklessly damaged the community before has been replaced by a new kind of violence, a sacred violence that restores peace to the community. The idea of a separation between profane violence and sacred (or redemptive) violence begins to grow. The sense of a community that transcends the individual adds to the sacred nature of this murder. This murder is called the founding murder because it has such a significant influence on unifying and establishing the community.

DEVELOPMENT OF RITUAL, RELIGION AND MYTH

The screams of the victim fall silent.

The hands that murdered withdraw.

Mindless rage gives way to focused wonder.

As passion fades and reason returns, the significance of the event makes us think about the whole process. What caused this suffering? What were the events, actions and objects involved that lead up to this climatic end? These suddenly find new meaning in the presence of the lifeless body that brought life to the communal body. The many conflictual experiences are finally symbolized in the awful corpse: order that comes from chaos, peace that comes from violence, and death that brings life. The dread we experienced when facing our dead victim expands to include all the events and objects involved in the process.

We do not want the violence that destroyed our community to erupt again, and we do not want to suffer the same fate as our victim. How do we protect ourselves? What caused the victim to suffer this punishment? Because we are unwilling to see ourselves as the cause of the victim's suffering we look for other causes. In our blind suspicion we soon identify the causes of the victim's fate: the *actions, words* and *objects* that defiled the victim and caused purity to demand revenge. The corpse is the first and most universally revered source of defilement. But the associated objects and actions that result in the corpse soon become "taboos" as well. Consequently a great diversity of taboos are developed in different religions. What might be sacred in one, is meaningless in another. What gives an object sacred status is determined by its presence in the events that lead up to the final violence. Consequently, there is a great diversity in religious practices, yet the actual practice of sacrifice is universal. Communities might have great diversity in their reasoning and speculation about caused these events, but in rage and violence they are all the same.

Obviously there is no one historic moment that we can refer to for the events just described, but the accumulation of memories of many such events eventually lead to the corpse becoming a sign. The meaning of the sign is re-enacted in our rituals and finds expression in language.

The profound effect that the sacrificial murder has upon the community demands explanation. *"The whole history of suffering cries out for vengeance and calls for narrative."* [7]

We cannot deny the unifying effect, the reconciliation and peace that these events bring to our communities, yet the deeply disturbing nature of the violence of the event stares us in the face. For the sake of the survival of our communities we need to justify this *redemptive* violence that brought an end to the destructive violence. And so the very victims that we at first demonized, we then begin to divinize. Rituals and stories explaining the rituals develop. "*Myths are the retrospective transfiguration of sacrificial crisis, the reinterpretation of these crises in the light of the cultural order that has arisen from them*"[8]

Origin myths typically begin with chaos. They recall a state of undifferentiation, where the differences that bring order to our world are dissolved. This is exactly what escalating violence did to early communities - it brought them to a crisis of distinction. Central to these myths is an act of redemptive violence. The chaos, the profane violence, is stopped by a creative and redemptive act of violence. The monsters depicted in these stories often have physical deformities and handicaps or they are the most beautiful of the community. These are typical characteristics of scapegoats: someone that is a bit different.

Because the whole process is one of symbols and changing representations, the horror of what is actually happening is swallowed up in sacred awe. The murder of an innocent

---

8   René Girard, Violence and the Sacred, Page 64.

victim becomes heroic sacrifice. The stories grow: stories about angry gods who delight themselves in blood, who restore the peace in exchange for sacrifice. Stories about guilty scapegoats. Blind to the mimetic nature of their own desires communities develop fantastic myths to explain what they cannot understand.

At the first sign of disorder within these newly formed communities, people who are caught up in magical thinking resort to the single victim mechanism to rid themselves of the evil. Many models are developed to explain this exchange, but in essence it remains a transaction with a god or gods to whom we are indebted. Ritual becomes the mimetic repetition of the founding murder.

TRANSFORMATION OF THE SCAPEGOAT

As religions develop out of the ritual, a need arises to make the horror of sacrificial murder more acceptable. Often, the victims themselves are persuaded of the necessity of their sacrifice. Parents, sincerely believing in the power of sacrifice, would persuade their child that the gods required his or her life. Our myths try to hide either the suffering or the innocence of the victim. In describing a ceremonial ritual of child sacrifice, Jean-Pierre Dupuy, observes the following:

> *The mother caresses the child so that he does not moan,*
> *witnesses do not weep or cry out of fear of compromising*

the dignity of the ceremony, and so on. Nor does the victim consider himself a victim, since his mother has handed him over to the priest, and since he has been made to understand that his sacrifice is necessary to appease the wrath of the god.[9]

And so the victim is transformed into a willing and heroic sacrifice.

ANCIENT FOUNDATIONS OF CIVILIZATION

Long after the establishment of these early societies, our more modern civilizations remained bound by the myth and violent mechanisms on which they were founded. Empires, sincerely believing in their divine right to domination, would teach their slaves, from the Bible, that slavery is God's will and purpose. Nations, believing in their divine right to luxury, would persuade their young men to sacrifice themselves in wars to guarantee "our way of life".

We convince ourselves that our victims either deserved their fate, or that they heroically volunteered to sacrifice themselves in order to wash our hands of their blood.

When the suffering of our sacrificial victims is acknowledged we can no longer hide the horror of what is happening. When the sacrifice is exposed as a victim, rather than a hero, the very foundations of the system start to crumble.

9   Dupuy, Jean-Pierre (2013-10-30). The Mark of the Sacred (Cultural Memory in the Present) (Kindle Locations 2085-2087). Stanford University Press. Kindle Edition.

When the innocence of our victims and the guilt of the community is revealed, we no longer have a legitimate reason for their slaughter.

WHAT HAPPENS IN REALITY?

People lose sight of the God who loves them.

In the absence of our true model, we begin to reflect one another's confusion and desires. Conflict escalates. Accusation thrives. The satan (accuser) stirs up chaos and drives the group to the point of destruction. The same process of accusation also finds a solution to the chaos by means of the single victim mechanism. This is "satan casting out satan".[10]

People lost in their quest to fulfill desires that they do not even know the origin of, form a mob and expel or murder an innocent victim. Their frustrations have been expressed in the most vile and violent form. They have killed their substitutionary rival, and for the moment they experience peace... a very fragile peace, for the real cause of their conflict has not been identified.

Shortly after, tension begins to grow again and conflict begins to escalate, for they have not dealt with the source of the conflict. No one wants the conflict to escalate to the point of destroying the community. When violence begins to escalate out of control, they remember what solved the

---

10   Luke 11:18, Matthew 12:26

problem the last time - a sacrifice! And so the founding murder is re-enacted in ritual. The ritual becomes a religion and religion becomes the foundation for a new culture. Laws that prohibit profane violence begin to develop. Religion is therefore born from violence and becomes the means by which violence is controlled.

What makes this mechanism so successful is the fact that it works so well. It unites communities, and human collaboration has untold benefits. However, despite the great success of sacrificial violence, it also comes at a great cost. Violence is never finally eradicated by violence. An evil empire might be overthrown by a better new empire, but if violence was used to do so, violence remains a threat to the new empire. A cycle of chaos and order, profane and sacred violence remains the best this system has to offer. The fact that something works does not mean it is right or that it is best. Sacrificial violence made human civilization possible, but is it the best way to be human and build community?

SCRIPTURE, HUMAN ORIGINS AND VICTIMS

Many only look at the Adam and Eve narrative for an understanding of human origins. But if we include the stories up to and including the flood, a much more comprehensive picture emerges of the fundamental human problem and of a society very much like our own. The question of original sin can so easily digress into just another way of shifting blame. The question becomes much more useful by rephrasing it. Instead of asking: "Who were the first humans to mess up and cause us all this suffering?" we can ask: "Who were the first humans to be like us; what was the first society that faced similar problems to our own?"

In the Genesis narrative, from Adam to Noah, we have the situation summarized as follows: The problem begins when mankind partakes of twisted mimetic desire - the acquisitive kind of desire that leads to rivalry. This results in broken human relationships. Nakedness is experienced as shame, for vulnerability is exploited to harm. Man rules over woman and mankind's relationship with creation becomes strained as well.

The Cain and Abel story has many of the characteristics of an origin narrative in its own right and consequently many scholars think it was a separate story that was woven into the Adam and Eve narrative. The point is that the story communicates more than just a sequential event. Cain and Abel are also the theological children of Adam and Eve. Violence is the offspring of twisted desire. This story further elaborates on the human condition when partaking of the wrong kind of desire and knowledge. The Hebrew scriptures also see the origin of human civilization in violence. The first murder, the first sin, the first sacrifice, and the first city are all mentioned in this one story of Cain and Abel. As with many myths that imagine a founding death as the beginning of their society, the scriptures also testify that the first civilization, the city of the Canaanites, was founded by Cain - the first murderer. What is unique about the Biblical account, compared to many mythical stories, is that there is no attempt to hide the innocence of the victim or guilt of the perpetrator. It simply says it as it is. Cain murdered Abel. And God hears the cries of the victim.

Civilization itself, our societal and cultural achievement, is implicated through this story. For if civilization had its origin in murder, it remains under threat of the sin that birthed it. In this story we see that God's warning "*you shall surely die*" was not a promise of external punishment, but an internal consequence of realizing the wrong possibility.

The story races on and we find Lamech - a man who killed a youth for striking him and then promises unlimited violence if anyone tries to take revenge. Violence continues to escalate. And so this theme of escalating violence leads us to the flood story.

> *The LORD saw that the wickedness of man was great in the earth, and that every intention of the thoughts of his heart was only evil continually. And the LORD regretted that he had made man on the earth, and it grieved him to his heart. So the LORD said, "I will blot out man whom I have created from the face of the land, man and animals*

*and creeping things and birds of the heavens, for I am
sorry that I have made them." But Noah found favor in
the eyes of the LORD.*

*These are the generations of Noah. Noah was a righteous
man, blameless in his generation. Noah walked with God.
And Noah had three sons, Shem, Ham, and Japheth.*

*Now the earth was corrupt in God's sight, and the earth
was filled with violence.*
(Genesis 6:4–11 ESV)

Note how evil intent and wickedness (verse 5) find their
fullest expression in violence (verse 11). Violence is not
necessarily blood and guts; it is any wrongdoing that harms
another. Here we see that all of creation has become subject
to corruption and the answer to this problem seems to
be nothing less than a whole new creation. As with many
ancient stories, the scriptures see violence as the most
pressing human problem. But unlike many of these stories it
begins to propose an alternative solution. The scapegoating
mechanism, whereby the community expels or murders the
minority, whereby the majority maintains their innocence
by projecting their guilt onto the scapegoat, is starting to be
exposed by the flood story. In this story the community is
guilty and the minority is innocent. Consequently it is the
whole community that dies while the minority escapes. It
is by no means a complete debunking of sacrificial myth,

but a new idea has been introduced: the majority is not necessarily right, and God might just be on the side of the minority!

The scriptures will continue to chip away at the myth of redemptive violence and maintaining order through sacrificial religion. They continue to tell stories from the victim's point of view.

God's dealings with Israel as a nation began while they were slaves! Usually the Empires recorded their stories of victory and conquest, but in what is considered one of the most important stories in scripture - the Exodus - it is the slaves whom God chooses as the center point of his story.

The aim of Empire is to maintain the status-quo and to justify their divine right to rule. The human dignity of slaves is something that the Empire is willing to sacrifice for its own glory. The Scriptures are surprising in that the story they tell is of a God who does not maintain the status-quo, but a God who makes all things new. Israel begins to see a God who is mindful of human suffering and ready to do something about it. The image of a patriotic God, a God on the side of the empire, is easily manipulated. Israel begins to see a God whose image cannot be manipulated. A God who identifies himself with victims is free from such manipulation. He continually threatens the stability of a society, a world, in which victims still exist.

The voices of victims grow stronger throughout the scriptures. Whether it be Joseph who is rejected by his brothers and falsely accused by Potiphar's wife, Job who protests his innocence, or the Psalmist that laments the suffering of the righteous, the scriptures are filled with the voices of victims who begin to transform our concepts of sacrifice.

Myths are not easily undone, especially because of their unconscious deceptive nature. A conversation needs to mature, a language needs to be developed and history needs to run its course for these stories to be concluded. In the context of sacrificial history, Jesus, who would become known as the last sacrifice, takes on a whole new meaning.

SUMMARY

This chapter was an introduction to Mimetic Theory. It is an enormous idea that contributes to almost every area of scientific inquiry within the social sciences. Hundreds of books have been written on the subject, so please don't feel discouraged if all the details are not clear to you yet. A chapter can at most only be an introduction to the idea. Maybe read this chapter again before proceeding.

In summary, we have traced the processes of desire from its personal mimetic origins to its social implications. Mimetic theory contemplates the very origins of human civilizations.

Twisted desire gives birth to conflict. Conflicts within communities often lead to the single victim mechanism.

These ancient origins of the practice of sacrifice are the beginning of ritual and religion, which in turn is the foundation for some of the first civilizations. However, being actors within this cycle of violence means that humans have been mostly blind to the processes that formed and sustained our societies. We also see how the scriptures begin to undo this blindness and question the most fundamental assumptions of the myths of sacred violence.

Humanity's difficult and violent past was very fruitful ground for endless stories that tried to make sense of the human situation. In the next chapter we'll explore the fascinating role that language plays in creating our reality.

PART 2 - DEVELOPING STORIES

5 - REFLECTIVE LANGUAGE

The human story is chaotic. There are moments of indescribable beauty and meaning, but it is also a story filled with twisted desire, conflict and violence. Our unique reflective abilities make us capable of the most intimate relationships, and simultaneously make us capable of the most horrific violence. But evil is not something we easily accept responsibility for. In fact it seems common for us to deal with evil by externalizing it and projecting it onto something or someone else.

This chaotic human story is replayed billions of times daily in individual lives. Individually we also find scapegoats to blame for our frustrations. We tell ourselves stories - personalized myths - in which we find guilty scapegoats, in which we imagine angry gods or visualize bad demons as the source of all our conflict. Let's now look at how language developed and how it functions to support the process of externalization.

Since time immemorial humanity has wondered, stood in awe, and speculated about the meaning of existence. We somehow sensed that there was a deeper meaning behind the visible, a greater value beyond the temporal, a story in the midst of the chaos. Language became the tool with which we mined for this treasure, with which we tried to extract the meaning and value out of existence. Our unique capacity to contemplate ourselves and the world around us, created the need for language to become ever more sophisticated and for literary forms to be sought with which to preserve our stories.

This is what makes us uniquely social creatures. We contemplate, we reflect, we find meaning... meaning beyond survival. It is this abundance of meaning that we communicate through our symbols. Some of the great apes have been taught the meaning of basic words. They know, for instance, that a.p.p.l.e. refers to a certain kind of fruit. But none could be taught the meaning of "you are the apple of my eye". They do not ask questions such as "Who am I?" or "What is the meaning of existence?" There is an excess of meaning in our symbolic language which is unique to humanity. Language is part of our unique ability to reflect our thoughts and feelings.

LANGUAGE AND THE CHAOS MONSTERS

Monsters and turbulent waters were used to symbolize chaos in the earliest stories ever told. In the Babylonian myth of Enuma Elish, it is Apsu and Tiamut who are the personifications of chaos - Apsu represented by sweet water and Tiamut by salt water. In Syrian myths it was Litan, the equivalent of the Hebrew Leviathan, another multi-headed sea-monster. It might have been the formless nature of water together with the fact that the depths of the seas were unexplored and unknown, that made these such apt symbols.

There is no doubt that the forces of nature were overwhelming to early man and often still are to modern man. However, I propose that the most chaotic and overpowering experience man first faced was not external, but it was the overload of information and the confusion that followed. It was not only the sensual stimulus that communicated an enormous amount of information about our environment, but also the addition of our internal mirroring capacity. By nature we reflect the desires of others and seek for intention behind all events. It is this capacity that leads to an excess of meaning in our journey to consciousness.

As man began to interpret the events around him, deconstructing all the impulses and seeking for meaning among the myriad of pictures all around, the original monster of chaos appeared: confusion! The overwhelming forces of nature reinforced the seemingly meaningless confusion. The way in which we began to slay this dragon was by reconstructing the meaning of events through narrative.

Remember, in chapter 2 we spoke about the different forms of *self*: the self of feeling, the self of action and the autobiographical self. The autobiographical self develops as we connect our memories by stitching different events together to find a common denominator. And what is more common to memories than the *self* that experienced them? We allow experiences to inform us about ourselves, and as a stronger sense of identity develops we reverse the teacher-student order by informing the experiences about their actual meaning. In order to preserve the sense of identity we have embraced, we reject any information that might contradict who we believe we are, thus adjusting our memories and even the whole storyline to confirm our underlying beliefs about ourselves.

Most people have used photographic software to adjust photos. Have you ever applied an artistic effect to a raw photo? These effects can be stunningly beautiful. Such adjustments require a lot of processing power from the device they run on in order to render the new image. In a similar way, human contemplation is the continual process, whether conscious or unconscious, by which we apply certain effects to the raw data we are constantly fed, in order to render a "movie" that makes sense. As we stitch all the images together we look for patterns, for a common thread that holds all the contradictions together. It seems that we do not enjoy contradictions, for in a way they contradict the one who experiences them. And we can't have that! We insist that all new information must confirm, or conform to, previous ideas. This seems to be the only way in which we can retain a stable sense of identity.

Our stories are the way in which we stitch together separate events to give them a meaning that they would never have on their own. These stories began as oral tradition and developed into a kind of communal memory. The values they taught became integral to the communities they were recounted in. They were told and retold, refined and adjusted, even reinvented to fit new situations. Understandably these stories became very dear, revered and even sacred. Some were eventually written down. Our narratives might have sincere and thoughtful origins, they may have formed our communities and influenced our individual identities, however, for us to progress we need to recognize them for what they are. Our stories have most often been simply projections of our own fears and confusion.

For us to discover greater meaning in our lives we have to be brave enough to dissemble the stories we currently believe... and that is scary because it means entering the formless waters of the unknown. It means letting go of certainty and facing the monster of chaos. But this is the only way in which we can retell our stories, by which we can reorder our life events and recognize value in them that we have not seen before.

LANGUAGE, TIME AND MEANING.

Is life simply a sequence of events... some boring, some exciting, some planned, some not? And do these events somehow form a meaningful story? Our time seems to be broken up into past, present and future. Is there any meaningful connection or value in these scattered pieces?

Time by itself is insubstantial. Time is simply a way of measuring movement. Twenty-four hours is a measurement of how long it takes the earth to spin around its axis, while 365 days is a measurement of how long it takes the earth to orbit the sun. Despite very imaginative movies that portray time as an actual dimension, reality as experienced in this universe means that time has no independent existence. Time is but a measurement of movement. The past is exactly that which no longer exists. The future is that which does not exist yet. Some therefore argue that the only reality is the present... but what is the present? Is it a day, an hour, or perhaps a second? The present is but the movement from a past that no longer exists into a future that does not yet exist. If time is simply the sequence of events it has no lasting substance, and therefore cannot give substance or value to our lives.

We need more than time to give meaning to our lives. We need something with which to embrace the scattered pieces of our past, present and future and make it a coherent whole - a way of finding our story within the chaos. There is a way of extracting the meaning of the moment and preserving it beyond its temporal existence - a means of extracting eternity from time. Narrative is the way in which we connect events, the means by which we capture their value and persist this value beyond the temporal.

Every day we encounter a deluge of events. Some we hardly notice, others deeply impact us. However, no event continues to exist as an objective reality. It is our experience of the event that remains a while longer... and our experiences are as unique as we are. Two people experiencing the exact same event might have very different experiences because each one interprets the event differently. Events are perceived, deconstructed by our understanding, reformed by our imaginations and occasionally reconstructed by our language.

Time, therefore, has its most real existence within our perception. The only way in which your past still exists is in your memory. The only way in which your future exists is in your anticipation. The only way in which the present exists is in your awareness.

The word 'spirit' is often used to describe this faculty of understanding. In many languages 'spirit' originates from, or is equivalent to, 'breath' or 'wind'. It's that unseen, immaterial, yet real force that moves and affects. The spirit of man is that part of you that is more than the sum total of your physical attributes, more than your bones and flesh. It's that part which gives understanding, the part that participates in creating your reality.

Our ability to interpret events means that the reality we live in is not a reality that exists objectively and independently but a reality we participate in through our perception. And therein lies the potential for great sorrow and great joy: the way in which we interpret the meaning of these events. The significance and value of these happenings might have been completely overlooked. Equally, there are many events, to which you might have assigned value… a value they never really possessed. We all, therefore, to a large extent, live in the reality of our own illusions. A large source of joy lies dormant under layers of anxious perceptions.

LANGUAGE AND COMMUNITY

It was the very impact of human experiences, the perception of their significance, that gave rise to the development of language. Language did not develop in isolation, but within a community of people sharing a common life or culture. Words became the means by which we exchanged thoughts and ideas. Communities experienced events so significant that they wanted to preserve and share them... or experiences so disturbing that they wanted to deny and hide them. Language developed for this very purpose: to share the beauty or to hide the shame of what we encountered.[1]

As we saw in the previous chapter, Anthropology reveals a history of barbaric violence and desperate attempts to justify and conceal our violent beginnings. We have a history of indescribable cruelty exceeded only by our collective self-deception in which we try to deny it. "... *human culture is predisposed to the concealment of its origins in collective violence.*"[2]

The stories we have told about ourselves and about God have mainly been tragedies. In our attempt to cover the tragedies, our words became twisted. Instead of using our words to reveal the beauty and value all around, they became tools to conceal the violence and obscure evil. Humanity's story, whether recorded in religious scripts, mythology or historic records, is one of confusion, guilt, violence, perversion, pain and a desperate search to move beyond this confusion.

Nothing can fill events with more meaning than love and violence. Often, violence has been the easier way to attach

---

1   In 'The Genesis of Secrecy' Frank Kermode shows how some narratives aim to obscure rather than illuminate.

2   René Girard, The Scapegoat, p100

significance to an event. Language itself was forged in the furnace of humanity's confusion - a humanity that lost sight of God and therefore forgot who they really were. As our mimetic capacity became twisted and produced all kinds of evil, even our language became perverted. Our inability to recognize the source of this evil, our unconscious projection of evil onto scapegoats, also found opportunity in our language to explain and simultaneously hide our greatest evils under the masks of the most sacred stories. And so ritual and myth, religion and manipulation, sacred scripture and hypnotic deception, have always gone hand in hand.

TIME BECOMES HUMAN

So, language is the symbols we use to describe our perceptions of reality, whether it's the external realities we observe or the internal realities we experience. We use language as an artist uses paint to capture pictures that will remain beyond the temporal scene we are describing. Internally, memory connects the images and so gives a sense of continuity. Language is the tool we invented to preserve our experiences beyond their temporal existence and to assist memory. It's the way in which we attempt to make time persist a bit longer in order to capture the significance of an event beyond its shadowy existence.

Our words become stories and our stories sustain our memories ... memories that attempt to keep in existence the actual events, feelings and thoughts that are no more. Language is the means by which we capture these temporal events and extract their meaning in order to sustain them beyond the moment.

> *We are no longer the same; our self has become transformed. The memory that ties together these successive states, along with the forgetfulness that conceals from us the origin of our desires, apparently permits us to believe in the underlying continuity of a permanent identity.*[3]

There is an underlying motivation in preserving memories that goes largely unnoticed. Our consciousness of *self* is constantly changing, but seeks stability. Self, which is constantly constructed and deconstructed, finds a sense of greater permanence in memory.

OUR STORIES, OUR REALITY

A bird catches a fruit fly.
So swift to die.
The fly, consumed,
is now transformed,
existing as the bird.

Time, more fleeting than a fruit fly,
A snapshot in our mind's eye,

---

3   Oughourlian, Jean-Michael (2009-12-15). The Genesis of Desire (Studies in Violence, Mimesis, & Culture) (Kindle Locations 674-676). Michigan State University Press. Kindle Edition.

is caught by our perceptions,
events, swallowed in our reflections,
by our language, reformed
by our stories, transformed.

Of time, all that remains,
all that it gains,
are our enduring stories,
preserving the essence of our memories,
narratives, in which do meaning dwell.
Tell them well.

Tell them with gratitude and joy,
transforming even moments of pain
that sought to destroy,
into memories of gain.

Time compressed,
the reality that remains,
are the stories we believe.

Time becomes human when the events we experience are processed by our perceptions, deconstructed by our imaginations, and reconstructed into meaningful and coherent stories.[4] Long after the reality we describe has passed away, our stories, our symbols, remain... and with them a sense of identity largely built upon these narratives.

---

4   For further reading on the relation of time and narrative, see Paul Ricoeur, Time and Narrative, Volume 1, Page 52

With the passage of time, these word pictures begin to take on a life of their own and drift ever further from the actual events they once described. Consequently, we have often confused our symbols with the experiences they once portrayed. Nowhere is the confusion between reality and the language we use to describe reality, more acute than in religious text.

LIMITATION OF LANGUAGE

...experiences without expression are blind, expressions without experience are empty. [5]

As language moves ever further away from the actual experience, it becomes more empty of reality, more deceitful. Once language has taken this turn, once it becomes a means of masking the actual event by avoiding the original experience, nothing is able to expose its deceit except returning to the actual experience.

SUMMARY

What a gift language is! It allows us to connect with each other; it enables us to break out of our isolating spaces and express what would have remained hidden.

Language gives us the ability to peer deeper into reality than what is plainly visible and as such find meaning, beauty and the opportunity to share our thoughts with others.

---

5   Jurgen Moltmann. The Spirit of Life (Kindle Location 355). Kindle Edition.

With language we not only reflect reality, we participate in shaping it for ourselves and others.

However, as with our reflective nature, language can be used for the greatest good or twisted for the greatest evil. In the chapter that follows we will examine some of the oldest stories humanity has told, and discover two very different trains of thought.

6 - Scripture Conversing with Myth

The Birthplace of the Bible

The Middle East is the source of many ancient texts including some of the oldest that date back thousands of years before Christ - much older than any Biblical documents we have: The Epic of Gilgamesh, Enuma Elish, The book of the Dead, to name a few. These stories include myths of creation, monsters of chaos, gods giving birth to other gods, floods, plaques and divine beings having intercourse with humans.

As we have already seen, although these stories are filled with imaginative monsters and wild speculation about the causes of chaos, they nevertheless have their origin in real events. The underlying themes of disruptive violence that is overcome by sacred violence have their beginning in real events. *"Myth constitutes the first major transition from experience to language."*[1]

This environment became the birthplace of the Hebrew Bible. As such the Bible has deep roots within the cultures

1   Paul Ricoeur. Figuring the Sacred: Religion, Narrative and Imagination (Kindle Locations 3703-3704). Kindle Edition.

and stories of the region. The Biblical stories have similar themes often following the same structure and containing many identical elements as the myths, however, the Bible radically changes the core message and proposes a whole new understanding. Many of its stories, therefore, use the myth genre to subvert the message of myth.

ORAL TRADITION

The ancient Middle Eastern civilizations were oral cultures, with literacy being the privilege of a few elite. Consequently, many of the recorded stories had ancient oral traditions. When they were eventually written down, it was predominantly in support of the oral traditions. In other words, texts were not written to be read in the modern sense of the word, they were written to be performed orally.

> *The native verbs for "reading" literally mean "to cry, to speak out loud" (Hebrew gdrd', Akkadian sasu and its by-form sitassu). These verbs reflect the way texts were used. Written documents were read aloud, either to an audience or to oneself. Silent reading was highly unusual. Even the student who read in solitude "muttered" his text (Ps 1:2; compare Acts 8:30). So when someone was urged to read something assiduously, the phrase was that he should not allow the text "to depart from his mouth" (Josh 11:8).15 Reading, in other words, was an oral activity.*[2]

---

2   Karel van der Toorn. Scribal Culture and the Making of the Hebrew Bible (Kindle Locations 162-165). Kindle Edition.

How each of the books in the Bible came to be in their present form involves a very rich and diverse history. The Bible is not a single book with a single author and a single message. It is a library of documents written in different styles and genres by different scribes and authors, for different reasons and to different audiences over an extended period of time. Their ideas developed over time and the authors did not always agree with each other. They were involved in a very lively debate about God, man, creation and the relations between them. These arguments were given voice in many oral traditions and diverse texts long before they were gathered and edited into one sacred entity.

Each document within this library called the Bible sounds a unique note in this symphony of reflection. There are patterns of recurring ideas and these ideas develop over time. The scriptures are rich conversations that move to and fro, forward and backward with ideas that develop and regress, but there is an overall direction or trajectory. It is this trajectory that we will follow in the chapters to come. It takes all of the scriptures to work through the confusion and fears that we projected onto God to get to the point where we can hear God speak clearly in the person of Jesus Christ.

SOURCES AND AUTHORS

The few books of the Hebrew bible that we have is a small part of what was a much larger literary library that no longer exists. The scriptures themselves are not shy in referring to other literary works for validation and inspiration! References include: "the Book of the Wars of the Lord" and "the Book of Jashar". In fact more than 20 external sources are mentioned by name in the Old Testament alone, all of which are lost to us.

Our modern idea of *author* was non-existent during the time in which these writings were produced. There was no market for literature as we know it today and documents were mostly produced by scribes to reflect the ideas of a group - not the ideas of individuals. A scribal class, working within religious or governmental institutions was largely responsible for producing documents. Karel van der Toorn identified 6 ways in which scribes produced these texts: "*They may engage in (1) transcription of oral lore; (2) invention of new text; (3) compilation of existing lore, either oral or written; (4) expansion of an inherited text; (5) adaptation of an existing text for a new audience; and (6) integration of individual documents into a more comprehensive composition.*"[3]

3　　Karel van der Toorn. Scribal Culture and the Making of the Hebrew Bible (Kindle Locations 1292-1293). Kindle Edition.

These biblical stories which often began as oral traditions, a kind of tribal memory, can be traced back to two distinct regions: The Northern Kingdom of Israel and the Southern Kingdom of Judah.

The first clue we get to support this view of multiple sources is in the text itself. It is not that obvious in our translations, but in Hebrew it is very noticeable that two different names are used for "God", namely, Elohim and Yahweh. Throughout the Pentateuch (first 5 books of the Bible) we often have two versions of a story, and in the different versions the different names for God are used. There are two creation stories, two stories of the Abrahamic covenant, two versions of how Isaac was named, two stories in which Abraham claimed that his wife Sarah was his sister, two versions of Jacob's journey to Mesopatamia and many more such doublets.

The two creation stories also use different names for God. The first creation story (Gen 1:1 – 2:4) uses Elohim. The second creation story (Gen 2:4-25) uses Yahweh Elohim. From chapter 4 onwards, Yahweh is used on its own. In our English Bibles, Yahweh is translated Lord. For many years I simply read the two creation stories as complementary, both giving different perspectives of the same events. However, not only do these two stories use different names for God and different styles of language, but there are also some definite contradictions. In the first creation story, Elohim creates plants first, then animals and finally mankind, both male and female. In the second creation story, Yahweh creates man first, then plants a garden and places man in this garden. After this he creates animals because he did not want man to be alone, and lastly, woman is made.

There were at least two very distinct sources from which the final text was constructed. There is a whole literary science called Source Criticism that divides the sources into J, E, D, and P. The Yahwist source is represented by J, the Elohist source by E, the Deuteronomist source by D and the Priestly source by P. [4]

Although the basic theory of such separate "sources" has been attacked again and again, and has been much revised, it remains in broad outline the basis of all modern literary critical and historical study of the Hebrew Bible. [5]

Some might argue that there is nothing unusual about referring to God by two different names. But there are many other differences as well. The E source also refers to the mountain of God at Horeb, whereas the J source calls it Mount Sinai. Moses' father-in-law is named Jethro by the E source but Reuel by the J source. When one divides the E and J stories, a pattern occurs that cannot be ignored. The E authors are consistently concerned with Israel and the J

4   Who Wrote The Bible, Richard Elliott Friedman
5   William G. Dever. What Did the Biblical Writers Know and When Did They Know It?: What Archeology Can Tell Us About the Reality of Ancient Israel (Kindle Locations 1253-1254). Kindle Edition.

authors with Judah and their interests were very different. Each wanted to prove their supremacy over the other and often told stories of the opposing kingdom that were not flattering at all.

Over time Yahweh and Elohim became identified with one another as these kingdoms tried to unify and as their monotheistic theology developed. This is further explored in chapter 9, *Mystery of God*, where we will trace the development of their conceptions of God.

And why is all this important to know?
Ancient Israelites were subject to the same influences as all other tribes. It is because they were typical that they were able to speak in a relevant way to the surrounding nations. Their ancient origins contain the same myths and primitive rituals, but the scriptures record the journey in which they progressively undo those myths. I intend to show the progression of scriptural thought by demonstrating how these writings entered into conversation with other ideas, often correcting and changing their own historic ideas.

GENESIS CREATION NARRATIVE VS ENUMA ELISH

An understanding of the literary and cultural environment in which the Genesis origin stories were produced can deepen our appreciation of their message.

The general agreement between scholars is that the Pentateuch is the end result of a complex process that included both oral and written traditions. The process of gathering the sources and intentionally committing them into the form that we know today began about 1000 BC with the monarchy of David. It continued until at least 500 BC which is after the exile to Babylon. The Babylonian exile demanded a response and is seen as prompting a significant rethinking of theology. Some scholars even argue for a date as late as 100 BC. So the Hebrew scriptures as we know them today only came into existence, at the earliest, around 500 BC.[6]

We know that Israel was in exile in Babylon between 586 BC – 530 BC. We also know that Enuma Elish was one of the most important myths of this time and was an integral part of Babylonial society, politics and religious cult. However, the myth was a part of the Middle Eastern region long before then. Copies have been found dating back to thousands of years BC. It is therefore highly likely that the authors of the Genesis creation accounts knew the story of Enuma Elish. As scholarly elite, they probably studied it. These speculations on their own might not carry much weight for some, but as we begin to examine the actual text I believe you will see significant similarities... which will make the differences all the more important.

---

6   W. Brueggemann, Theology of the Old Testament: Testimony, Dispute, Advocacy, 74-75

Jewish teachers often used myth in order to debunk myth. Familiar entities and story lines were employed to propose the very opposite ideas of what the original myth declared.

Enuma Elish

As we examine this myth and the part it played in daily life, imagine what influence it would have on one growing up with this story. Imagine the view it gave of the gods, man and the world. It might be very foreign to our ears but in a world plagued by violence and natural disasters - a world seemingly empty of meaning or hope - myth played a powerful role in restoring meaning and helping people peer into the mysteries of our existence.

For us to perceive the radical new message of Genesis 1, we need to understand that in the context of the Babylonian exile, Enuma Elish was the story it competed with. Enuma Elish takes its name from the first few words of the myth, *"When on high"*

> *When on high the heaven had not been named,*
> *Firm ground below had not been called by name,*
> *Naught but primordial Apsu, their begetter,*
> *Mummu-Tiamat, she who bore them all,*
> *Their waters co-mingling as a single body;*
> *No reed hut had been matted, no marsh land had appeared,*
> *When no gods whatever had been brought into being,*

Uncalled by name, their destinies undetermined–;
Then it was that the gods were formed within them.

Here we have the original gods of chaos. Apsu, the divine male personification represented by sweet water, and Tiamat, the divine female personification represented by salt water. Through the co-mingling of their waters, a picture of sexual union, they brought forth divine offspring. These gave birth to another generation of gods, and so many generations of gods were born.

However, the generations of offspring became troublesome to Apsu and Tiamat, disturbing their rest with their noisy hilarity.

The divine brothers banded together,
They disturbed Tiamat as they surged back and forth,
Yea, they troubled the mood of Tiamat
By their hilarity in the Abode of Heaven.
Apsu, opening his mouth,
Said unto resplendent Tiamat:
"Their ways are verily loathsome unto me.
By day I find no relief, nor repose by night.
I will destroy, I will wreck their ways,
That quiet may be restored. Let us have rest."
Then answered Mummu, (Mummu Tiamat) giving counsel to Apsu;
(Ill-wishing) and ungracious was Mummu's advice:

"Do destroy, my father, the mutinous ways.
Then shalt thou have relief by day and rest by night."
When Apsu heard this, his face grew radiant
Because of the evil he planned against the gods, his sons.

And so Apsu and Tiamat plot to destroy their noisy offspring. (I imagine this was not a popular bedtime story.) However, their plan fails through the quick acting earth-water god, Ea. Apsu is killed and Tiamat plans revenge. She spawns a whole new army to assist her. The gods are terrified. They need a leader – a hero that can save them from Tiamat's anger. Marduk appears as this hero, but he demands a high price: undisputed supremacy over the gods. The story perceives violence, deceit and murder to be the history of our cosmos. It is significant that evil chaos is present even before creation. Evil is perceived to be more original that the creator god, Marduk, himself. Man, therefore, is not responsible for this evil but simply discovers it and continues it.

His heart exulting, he said to his father:
"Creator of the gods, destiny of the great gods,
If I indeed, as your avenger,
Am to vanquish Tiamat and save your lives,
Set up the Assembly, proclaim supreme my destiny!
Let my word, instead of you, determine the fates.
Unalterable shall be what I may bring into being,

Neither recalled nor changed shall be the command of my lips.

The gods agree and empower Marduk with their spells. The war begins and the battle between Tiamat and Marduk is described as follows:

In fury, Tiamat cried out aloud,
To the roots her legs shook both together.
Then joined issue, Tiamat and Marduk,
They strove in single combat, locked in battle.
The lord (Marduk) spread out his net to enfold her,
The Evil Wind, which followed behind, he let loose in her face.
When Tiamat opened her mouth to consume him.
He drove in the Evil Wind that she close not her lips.
As the fierce winds charged her belly,
Her body was distended and her mouth was wide open.
He released the arrow, it tore her belly,
It cut through her insides, splitting the heart.
Having thus subdued her, he extinguished her life.
He cast down her carcass to stand upon it.

Of course my favorite line in the myth is: "*The Evil Wind, which followed behind, he let loose in her face.*" Have we not all had problems with an "*evil wind that followed behind us*", but Marduk shows extraordinary talent by killing a monster with his!

The monster of chaos is defeated through a wind that Marduk let loose in her face. He then continues to split her body in two and creates the universe from it. One half becomes the firmament above (the heaven) and the other becomes the firmament below (the earth). Do elements of the story sound familiar?

He split her like a shellfish into two parts.
Half of her he set up and sealed it as sky,
Pulled down the bar and posted guards.
He bade them to allow not her waters to escape.

Then Marduk starts using his sovereignty to assign tasks to the other gods. The tasks however, soon become exhausting to them. To give them some relief Marduk uses the blood of the slain commander of Tiamat's army, Kingu, to create mankind.

Blood I will mass and cause bones to be.
I will establish a savage, "man" shall be his name,
Verily, savage man I will create.
He shall be charged with the service of the gods
That they might be at ease.
They bound him, holding him before Ea.
Out of (Kingu's) blood they fashioned mankind
Ea imposed the service and let free the gods.

Mankind is therefore created as an afterthought, invented for servitude, and our very beginning is perceived to be in the blood of violence. As an expression of their gratitude the gods build Marduk a temple in Babylon called Babel, which means "the gate of the god".

What was the meaning of the myth and what influence did it have within the Babylonian community in which Israel were present as exiles? For these people myth was not simply an imaginative story, it was a reality that they lived out in cult rituals. It described the relations between the gods and how that affected man.

MIMETIC CONFLICT AS THE ORIGIN OF MYTH

First we must consider the myth in the context of Mimetic theory: As with many origin myths, Enuma Elish recalls a state of chaos where differentiation disappears in a formless body of water. Disorder within the community of the gods gives rise to escalating violence. The natural boundaries between parents and their offspring disintegrates as the parents (Apsu & Tiamat) plot to kill their offspring, and the offspring plot to replace their parents. Rivalry within the family reaches a boiling point where all the gods fear total annihilation. At this moment, a single entity is identified as the source of all their trouble: Tiamat. A single enemy is the first element needed to unite the gods, but it is only after Tiamat is violently destroyed that the unity reaches its highest point and all the gods unanimously sing the praises of Marduk. The creative act of Marduk, in which he distinguishes, separates, and orders the body of Tiamat, is inseparable from the violence with which he murders her. The confusion of good and evil, a knowledge that mixes both good and evil, is so clearly displayed here. It is the wind that brings deliverance from evil waters - a theme that we'll see repeated in the scriptures as well. Order is restored through violence. Violence is glorified as the means by which the community is renewed and united. The creation of mankind from the blood of Kingu also testifies to this. Humanity is born from violent blood, there is therefore no way to escape this condition. Can you see how compatible this myth is with the actual events of a community in crisis and the processes of mimetic realism?

THEOGONIC

The myth is theogonic, meaning, it gives an account of how and where the gods came from. Evil is perceived as so basic to our cosmos that the gods themselves have their origin in overcoming this chaos. The co-mingling of Apsu and Tiamat's waters implies a sexual act. It seems like sexual union was the only way in which the origin of gods could be imagined.

The idea that there is a realm (the primordial waters) beyond the gods is also very important, as it will give birth to many magical practices in which people tried to access this realm to which even the gods are subject. Over time, the gods become identified with natural phenomena. There is the storm god, the wind god, the fertility god, etc. And because there are many gods, no one god's will is absolute. It can be opposed and thwarted by another.

There is also nothing particularly moral about the gods. There is no reason to expect a god to act justly. They can be involved in all kinds of immoral and violent acts. At times they can act kindly as well, but they are essentially amoral. In short, they have very human characteristics. The desires, feelings, rage and violent actions - the evil man recognizes in himself - is identical to what is ascribed to the gods.

COSMOLOGICAL

The myth was also an attempt to tell people why our world is the way it is. It not only explained the origin of our community, but the cosmos itself. Above us and below us are chaotic waters. The body of Tiamat, split in half, provides protection from these waters. If the upper firmament body develops holes, it leaks and so we have rain. If the lower firmament body leaks, we have springs, etc. The sun and moon are stations for the gods. For us it might be a very crude explanation, but it was one of the first attempts to tell the community why the universe works the way it does. The fact that the gods were amoral and identified with natural forces explained why this world could be such a hostile environment.

SOCIAL AND POLITICAL

The hierarchy of gods and humans in Enuma Elish corresponds to the social structures in Babylon at that time.

The position of slaves corresponds to the creation of man. Their purpose is to serve. The gods don't have much interest in humanity, except that humanity should serve them. Humanity does not have much inherent value; we were more of an afterthought. Marduk's history also resembles the history of a certain Babylonian king who rose as a fairly unknown king to this supreme position known as "*the king above all gods*". The political and religious elite correspond to the positions of the gods.

The recurring theme of redemptive violence is prominent in Enuma Elish. The way in which order is brought out of chaos and the way in which order is maintained, is through violence. The message is clear – if there is disorder in your country, in your city or in your home, use whatever force necessary to bring it back into order. It is evident that these stories were used to affirm and reinforce the status-quo. Sacred text became a very useful way to manipulate the population to accept the order created by the Empire and turn a blind eye to the suffering and the victims that were strewn along the way.

It will be seen that human violence is thus justified by the primordial violence. Creation is a victory over an Enemy older than the creator; that Enemy, immanent in the divine, will be represented in history by all the enemies whom the king in his turn, as servant of the god, will have as his mission to destroy. Thus violence is inscribed in the origin of things, in the principle that establishes while it destroys.[7]

Cult Rituals

Myth was not simply an abstract story, but represented actual events that continued to influence the present. Because evil was understood to be older than creation itself, the battle between good and evil was therefore eternal. The cold dark wintery season made the combat between life and death so tangible. Seasonal rituals mimetically re-enacted these battles between life and death, chaos and order. The participants believed that they were actually part of rejuvenating nature. This sense of magical connection to creation made these rituals very relevant and valuable to those involved.

Myths, then, in the final analysis, have as their subjects the eternal problems of mankind communicated through the medium of highly imaginative language. A myth may be a vital cultural force. It can be a vehicle for the expression of ideas that activate human behavior, that reflect and validate the distinctive forms and qualities of a

---

7   The Symbolism of Evil, Paul Ricoeur, page 182

civilization, that signify a dynamic attitude to the universe and embody a vision of society.[8]

GENESIS REPLY

Within its literary context, the Genesis origin narratives are brilliant replies to the popular stories of their day. I do not thereby mean that the sole motivation for writing the Genesis origin stories was to reply to the Enuma Elish myth, but it certainly was part of the reason. These Biblical narratives deliberately allude to the myths in order to subvert the very message they were meant to communicate.

Let's now look at Genesis and its radical new thought. The first sentence of Genesis is almost exactly the same as the first line of Enuma Elish. It might not be that apparent in our english translations, but lets look at it in more depth.

In the beginning ... (Genesis)
When on high ... (Enuma Elish)
The word 'began / beginning' is explained in the
Theological Wordbook of the Old Testament as follows:
first, beginning, best.
The primary meaning of this root is "head." It is common to all Semitic languages and appears in its root forms and derivatives nearly 750 times. ... It is used also for the top or summit of a geographical feature such as a mountain or hill (17:9) and the upper part of a building or architectural

8   Sarna, Nahum M. (2014-01-06). Understanding Genesis (The Heritage of Biblical Israel) (Kindle Locations 506-509).

feature (Gen 11:4; 2 Chr 3:15) and as a personification for such features (Ps 24:7, 9)

Those who were familiar with the Enuma Elish story would immediately have recognized the same starting sentence in the Genesis story.

When on high (at first) … there was water and chaos, then something happened.
It is very similar to Gen 1: When God began to create… the earth was void and without form.

Many scholars agree that a better translation of Gen 1:1 would be: *"When God began creating …"* rather than *"In the beginning"*

You might be familiar with the concept of creation out of nothing (ex nillio). *In the beginning* implies that this is the first event in time. The Genesis narrative has often been used to support this concept as it seems to be speaking about the ultimate origins of the universe. Yet, something more is being communicated.

The wording "when God began creating" has a very different message. It speaks of a process in which God brings order to disorder, how God brings meaningful form to the unformed chaos. Its main concern is not to explore the scientific origins of the universe but rather to explain how God creates... and it is very different from any of the other stories. The world was a chaotic, formless place. God sends his wind into the face of the deep chaotic waters. Again, this would sound very familiar to those who knew the Enuma Elish story. Remember the battle between Marduk and Tiamat, the watery god of chaos? Marduk sends a wind into the face of Tiamat and destroys her. In the Genesis story we are again confronted with chaotic waters. God also uses a wind and sends it into the face of the deep. The Hebrew word "deep" is etymologically[9] the same word as Tiamat.

Professor Christine Hayes, in her lectures on Genesis at Yale University, says it this way:

> ...you should immediately hear the great similarities. Our story opens with a temporal clause: "When on high," "when God began creating"; we have a wind that sweeps over chaotic waters, just like the wind of Marduk released into the face of Tiamat, and the Hebrew term is particularly fascinating. In fact, the text says "and there is darkness on the face of deep." No definite article. The word "deep" is a proper name, perhaps. The Hebrew word is Tehom. It means "deep" and etymologically it's exactly the same word as Tiamat: the "at" ending is just feminine. So Tiam, Tehom–it's the same word, it's a related word. So, the wind over the face of deep, now it's demythologized, so it's as if

---

9   The study of the origin of words and the way in which their meanings have changed throughout history

they're invoking the story that would have been familiar and yet changing it. So the storyteller has actually set the stage for retelling the cosmic battle story that everyone knew. That was a story that surely was near and dear to the hearts of many ancient Israelites and Ancient Middle Eastern listeners, so all the elements are there for the retelling of that story. We've got wind, we've got a primeval chaotic, watery mass or deep, and then surprise, there's no battle. There's just a word, "let there be light." And the Ancient Middle Eastern listener would prick up their ears: where's the battle, where's the violence, where's the gore? I thought I knew this story. So something new, something different was being communicated in this story.[10]

Are you beginning to appreciate what the Genesis story was designed to do, how it draws from familiar themes but radically changes the content? It shares much in common with popular myths, but for all its points of similarity its most striking quality is its points of difference.

NEW VISION OF GOD

With pure elegance, the Genesis narrative introduces us to the God who simply is. Unlike the highly imaginative stories of the origins of the gods, the unpretentious language of Genesis boldly declares a God who needs no explanation, who has no other-worldly history. He is as evident as creation itself, yet remains mysteriously beyond and above creation. As the 13th century Franciscan St. Bonaventure said: "*God is an intelligible space whose center is everywhere and circumference is nowhere... God is within all things, but not enclosed, outside all things but not excluded, above all things but not aloof, below all things but not debased... God is supremely one and all inclusive, God is therefore 'all-in-all'.*"

This God is beyond comparison and without competition. There is no evil that precedes him. He is therefore not caught up in our cycle of rivalry. The gods of Enuma Elish are as deeply involved in violent rivalry as humanity and therefore they cannot offer a way out of it. But the Elohim of Genesis does not rely on violence to be creative, instead his creativity is expressed in a word. He speaks and brings distinction. The quintessence of his self-giving is displayed as he gives his very image and likeness, his own self in man. This is the very inverse of the self-centered, glory-seeking, violent and withholding Marduk.

Even his most exclusive characteristic as Creator is not an ability he withholds from his creation. Rather, as we've seen before, he invites creation to participate with him in realizing creative possibilities. And so he doesn't make plants and animals by himself and then just place them on earth. Rather, he speaks to the earth, the material from which plants and animals are made, and tells it to bring forth these creatures. His creation is given the freedom to participate in the creative act with him!

The God of Genesis has no dependence on violence to create. He brings order through the spirit of his word participating with his creation in realizing new possibilities. His creativity is expressed through his message. He has no desire to manipulate or control but gives his creation freedom.

Such a vision of God annihilates the very basis for magical practices. In the mythical world of Enuma Elish the gods have their origin in a prehistoric realm of chaotic waters. This meant that even the gods were subject to these magical elements. Incantations and magical potions made for great business in a world where people continually lived in fear of revengeful gods. (Superstitious practices are still very lucrative today, in religions founded on fear.) But the God of Genesis has no theogony, no realm or substance to which he is subject. *He cannot be manipulated!* He also has no competition. There are no storm-gods, water-gods or any other God that can contradict him. He speaks and it is done. Creation is not in any way in competition with this God, but exists through God. God may well express himself in natural forces, but they are not equal to him. The whole basis for magic is being exposed and brought to nothing. The superstitions of natural forces being the personifications of different gods are being exposed as groundless. The Genesis scriptures were radically new in that they were in fact, demythologizing literature. Their aim was to set people free from religious superstitions that caused constant anxiety.

A very important difference between the God of Genesis and the mythical gods is that Elohim is fundamentally good. The gods of myth are amoral. Like humans they can be good and evil, just and unjust. But the God of Genesis is only good. With rhythmic repetition all his creative acts are declared to be good! The world he creates is not amoral, it is good. A good God has enormous implication for human life. It means that we have something and someone to rely on. We can expect this God to consistently act in a certain way. And if God is just, then the way we live, matters. He is not necessarily on the side of our family, our tribe, our empire. He is on the side of truth, mercy and justice. The consequences are enormous for civilizations that claim God as the one who supports whatever they do. This God cannot be manipulated for political purposes. Rather, our politics will need to answer to the God who values all of creation. The goodness of God and of God's creation precede evil, which means that evil has a different beginning or entrance into this world.

New Vision of Mankind
With such a radically new vision of God, what it means to be human also radically changes. Whereas man was an afterthought in Enuma Elish, a by-product of twisted mimetic rivalry, the man of Genesis has his origin in the

creative self-giving God - in pure mimetic desire. The order of creation in Enuma Elish moves from the highest level, the gods themselves, to the lowest - mankind. In Genesis the order moves up towards the crescendo, from plants to fish and birds, to animals and lastly, the visible image of God - mankind. Far from being just pawns in the hands of greater forces, mankind has endless possibilities and freedom of being. In fact, man is even capable of resisting the one sovereign God!

In Enuma Elish, humanity's very origin is violence. In Genesis, mankind is the ultimate expression of the creative God who in no way depends on violence to be creative. Mankind has their beginning in the one who cannot be defined - the God of infinite possibilities. As his image and likeness, we are also beyond definition; we have infinite possibilities of being; we can be whatever we behold. Maybe it is possible for us to imagine a new way of being human, a new way of uniting our societies without the need for manipulation.

The gods of the myths are often portrayed as female monsters of chaos and male heroes who subdue them through violence. A male patriarchal God has many unwanted side effects. It affected the way women were valued and treated in society, and still does.

The God of Genesis is not exclusively male or female. In a society where males thought it their divine right to dominate, even with violence, the author of Genesis is introducing a radically new idea: God is no more favorable towards men than towards woman and he/she does not need violence to bring order to chaos.

GENESIS COSMOLOGY

To a large extent, the Hebrews shared a similar conception of the cosmos as their neighbors. There was a firmament above and beneath to keep the waters back. There were pillars keeping the skies and the earth in place. There were heavenly storehouses for rain and for hail, etc.

What was radically new in the Genesis account was that these natural forces were the creations of God and not competing gods. The immediate implication was that natural substances no longer had magical qualities. Previously a magical water potion could protect you against the fire god. But if there is only one sovereign God who made all creation good and through whom all things exist, then no potion can be used against him.

GENESIS - SOCIAL AND POLITICAL.

In one sense the Genesis narrative is nonpolitical. It does not try to validate Israel, Jerusalem or the Temple cult. But at the same time, its vision of God, man and creation is radically political because of the serious implications it has for the way in which we do society. In a society that was completely dependent on slavery the idea of all humans having equal value was extremely dangerous. It still is. Equal value does not imply uniformity. If anything it promotes and celebrates diversity.

A story that questions the hierarchy of society and removes violence as an acceptable way of ruling must have been the most shocking story the Babylonian population had ever heard. This is why it became one of the most enduring human stories. Israel was not the biggest or richest or most influential nation in the Middle East. What gave them such a huge influence on the world was that they had a new idea. A new idea about God, man and the world we live in. These ideas are still shaping the social and political landscapes of our world.

Summary

Different regions and different sources, had different interpretations of events and consequently told different stories. The Bible is therefore not a book that holds to any one theology - it contains multiple competing theologies in conversation with one another. Often these conversations were responding to the ethics, the historic situation, and the beliefs of its time and region. And so in it we see ideas develop.

We will look at five developing ideas in the chapters that follow. We will discover in the scriptures how events were re-interpreted and adjusted. On occasion, religious practices that were common and acceptable in earlier Israelite religion were later condemned and replaced.

It's a fascinating journey and even if you do not agree with the approach I trust you will find the journey informative. The five ideas we will explore are: the mystery of who God is, the changing story of sacrifice, the paradox of evil, the history of Satan, and the growing expectation for a coming Messiah.

7 - MYSTERY OF GOD

There have been many influences that have shaped mankind's ideas of the sacred. A few, though, seem to be universal. When apposing experiences are simultaneously present, the resultant wonder and awe gives birth to a sense of the sacred.

The beauty of nature can be tangible - the shapes and colors, the smells and textures, the enormous scale and intricate detail can bring one into an awareness of the closeness of God. Such experiences of the immanence (nearness) of God are also expressed throughout the scriptures. Job experiences the Spirit of God, not as a distant entity, but as the breath of life that permeates all of creation. In speaking of God, he says: "*In whose hand [is] the breath of every living thing, And the spirit of all flesh of man*" (Job 12:10 YNG). Job equates his own breath with the Spirit of God: "*the spirit of God is in my nostrils*" (Job 27:3 KJV). Although breathing creatures are more obviously given life by the breath/wind/spirit of God, the rest of creation is not excluded. "*By the breath of God frost is given: and the breadth of the waters is straitened*" (Job 37:10 KJV).

Additionally, the incomprehensible size of creation can be overwhelming. Looking up at the sky which seemed to go on forever, observing the majestic clouds, lightning, hail and rain, often evoked a sense of awe and inspired many of our earliest stories. Early references to the divine personifies the sky and speaks of the great sky God. Unlike the breath of life, the infinite sky gave a sense of God's transcendence.

However, nowhere do opposites become as intense and obvious as in the corpse of the scapegoat. The horror of violence and its deathly effect is positioned next to the beneficial peace that unites the community and restores the order. The corpse becomes the symbol of both curse and blessing. Our reflective nature, our identification with another human who became our victim, means that the experience is greatly intensified. The deeply disturbing nature of murdering one of our own and the profound influence that this violent deed has in unifying the community is undoubtedly a significant influence on our sense of the sacred. The chaos, the senseless and profane violence that was about to destroy a community, is overcome by this single act of "sacred" violence. This event of sacred violence was probably most influential in forming humanity's views of the gods, as it was the most significant factor in establishing and maintaining order within communities. The views and myths that develop from this brutal event are by far the most disturbing. Gods who delight in violence, blood and destruction are often the result of men basing their theories on the event of sacrifice. Sacrifice is also the influence that gives our myths a socio-political dimension. When social hierarchies become entangled with religious worship, perversion is inevitable. Worship then, is no longer the simple act of awe and wonder, but soon becomes a manipulated ritual. Religion becomes the exchange whereby the gods manipulate us and whereby we manipulate the gods and one another.

These experiences of the sacred give birth to an enormous diversity of stories as mankind tries to make sense of what they cannot understand. As each community develops their myths, rituals and religious traditions, a multitude of gods are created in the image and likeness of that particular community. When these communities interact their gods are sometimes perceived to be the same divine beings known by different names, but most often they are perceived as competing gods. This belief in many gods is referred to as polytheism. The belief in one God through whom all things exist is known as monotheism. The above definitions are admittedly oversimplified but will be expanded further in the pages to follow.

MANY GODS AND ONE GOD.

Why is this important? Has this issue not been settled long ago? To believe in many gods is ridiculous - there is only one true God… and obviously it's the one I believe in! Such naive statements make it appear that the only difference between the idea of multiple gods and this understanding of one God, is simply a number. The difference is profoundly greater.

Monotheism and polytheism are often portrayed as two apposing worldviews, but the relationship between them is rich and complex. There are, paradoxically, more similarities and greater differences than many believers realize.

DIFFERENCES

As with all ideas, monotheism developed and branched into a great variety of directions. However, those who have given the subject their attention see in monotheism much more than a belief in one supreme being. It is a completely new category of understanding God. Polytheistic gods were perceived as beings who existed very much as we do, however, with some special powers and privileges. God, however, does not exist as a being among other beings but rather is the One source from which all being and existence is sustained. Whereas the stories of the gods included fanciful accounts of their origins and histories, the One God of the Genesis narrative has no independent history but simply is as present as creation itself. Creation in this context is not a historic event, but something that happens moment by moment. The Creator in this context is not some demiurge[1] that performed the act of creation a long time ago but rather the indivisible and ever present reason why there is something rather than nothing.

SIMILARITIES

Many Christians also think that the belief in one supreme god began with the Hebrew people, and that the Hebrew scriptures were written by monotheists often in opposition to polytheists. However, polytheistic communities had a way of reconfiguring their theories to portray the unity of the divine. There has also always been something very 'poly' about Israel's monotheism. How these concepts compete, influence and complement one another is fascinating and very important for later Christian conceptions of what and who God is.

> *Several of the religious cultures that we sometimes inaccurately characterize as "polytheistic" have traditionally insisted upon an absolute differentiation between the one transcendent Godhead from whom all being flows and the various "divine" beings who indwell and govern the heavens and the earth. Only the one God, says Swami Prabhavananda, speaking more or less for the whole of developed Vedantic and Bhaktic Hinduism,*

---

1   a being responsible for the creation of the universe, in particular. (in Platonic philosophy) the Maker or Creator of the world. (in Gnosticism and other theological systems) a heavenly being, subordinate to the Supreme Being, that is considered to be the controller of the material world and antagonistic to all that is purely spiritual.

is "the uncreated": "gods, though supernatural, belong ... among the creatures. Like the Christian angels, they are much nearer to man than to God." Conversely, many creeds we correctly speak of as "monotheistic" embrace the very same distinction. The Adi Granth of the Sikhs, for instance, describes the One God as the creator of Brahma, Vishnu, and Shiva. In truth, Prabhavananda's comparison of the gods of India to Christianity's angels is more apt than many modern Christians may realize. Late Hellenistic pagan thought often tended to draw a clear demarcation between the one transcendent God (or, in Greek, ho theos, God with the definite article) and any particular or local god (any mere "inarticular" theos) who might superintend this or that people or nation or aspect of the natural world; at the same time, late Hellenistic Jews and Christians recognized a multitude of angelic "powers" and "principalities," some obedient to the one transcendent God and some in rebellion, who governed the elements of nature and the peoples of the earth . To any impartial observer at the time, coming from some altogether different culture, the theological cosmos of a great deal of pagan "polytheism" would have seemed all but indistinguishable from that of a great deal of Jewish or Christian "monotheism."[2]

---

2   Hart, David Bentley (2013-09-24). The Experience of God (pp. 29-30). Yale University Press. Kindle Edition.

Many isolated communities believed in one high God prior to any contact with western civilization including Pygmies, Fijians, and indigenous Australians. Many ancient communities, even prior to Israel's existence, show a belief in one supreme God including ancient Chinese and Persian communities. It is also significant to find traces of monotheism in Egypt around the time when Moses' story was busy unfolding. The Pharaoh Akhenaten introduced a form of monotheism in the 14th century BC. He also wrote a hymn, "Hymn to the Aten", containing a portion that is almost identical to Psalm 104. Subsequent rulers in Egypt reverted back to the traditional gods and tried to erase Atenism from Egyptian records.

So we can see that both monotheistic and polytheistic ideas were present in the region where Israel was being formed. However, polytheism was by far the more popular view and had a marked influence on early Israel. Israel did not begin their faith journey by believing in one supreme God, and that all other gods were false. In fact, this chapter will show that Israel, like every other tribal nation in their region, believed in many gods and that Yahweh was their tribal God. From this polytheistic background, their monotheistic theology grew and only culminated during their transition to monarchy.[3] The journey from polytheism to monotheism was a gradual

---

3   Mark S. Smith. Memoirs of God (Kindle Location 1526). Kindle Edition.

evolutionary process but also a revolutionary change as the very nature of God was redefined.

Regarding ancient Israel's polytheistic beginnings, I do not offer anything original in this chapter, except perhaps to show its origin in sacrificial violence and general conformity to mimetic theory. Ancient Israel's development from polytheism to monotheism has been part of academic discussion for decades as the recommended books for this chapter, make clear. Regarding the influences on this chapter, I am especially grateful for the writings of Mark S. Smith. What I do hope to accomplish, which I have not found in other writings, is to connect this theme with the other developing stories, and place them in the context of Mimetic Theory. This, in turn, will expand and enrich the context within which the message of Jesus can be understood. So please be patient, the significance and relevance of what it means to you personally, will become clearer in later chapters.

POLYTHEISM IN ANCIENT MIDDLE EAST.
STRUCTURE OF DIVINITIES.

Their are many types of polytheism, but the Mesopotamian and Canaan areas had much in common and are part of the larger cultural context to which Israel belonged. Our exploration of Polytheism will therefore be limited to this area. The text which is of particular interest, known as the

Ugaritic text, was found at what is known today as Ras Sharma in Syria, which lies just north of Israel.

Divinities were largely categorized into two groups: those who were beneficial and those who were destructive. The beneficial gods were portrayed with human characteristics or as domesticated animals such as bulls and goats, while the destructive gods were generally portrayed as monsters and wild animals such as snakes.

These gods also occupied different spaces that demonstrated their relationship to the community. Three spaces can be identified. First there was the center of the community. Then the periphery which was the space between the center and the unknown. Thirdly, that which lay beyond the periphery such as the underworld and the chaotic waters. Remember, in ancient cosmology the land is surrounded by water - around, below and above. These unknown formless waters were the abode of the destructive water monsters.

At the heart of these communities we find a patriarchal family unit. However the center also includes the wider community. It is the space in which we are safe - the familiar and civilized community in which we are at home. The beneficial gods were also at home in the center of the community. So a mountain or a high place within the boundaries of the community would often be set apart for these gods.

Foreign gods could be found at the periphery. These gods are acknowledged, even revered, but no cult or ritual exists within the community to honor such foreign gods. For example, the people of Ugarit acknowledged the gods of Egypt, but no sacred places are found within their boundaries to worship these gods.

Beyond the periphery is the dwelling place of the monsters. Death and chaos, represented by different names, roamed these areas. These monsters are able to express themselves through natural phenomena such as floods, storms, pestilence and whatever caused death.

DIVINE COUNCILS.

Within most of these polytheistic worldviews there existed the concept of divine councils, which in a way united all the gods under one most high God.

The Ugaritic text gives us some insight into how the divine councils were organized. Many of the gods it identifies by name are also found within Biblical text.

The groupings of the gods according to this text are as follows:

- At the highest level: El and his wife Athirat (Biblical Asherah)
- At the second level: The immediate family of El, often referred to as the sons of El. The sons of El

would often be in conflict with one another, vying for position and rank. These include Athtart and Athtar (the evening and morning star); Shapshu (sun) and Yarih (moon); Shahar (dawn) and Shalim (dusk); Resheph; also Baal, the warrior/storm-god.

- A possible third level existed, consisting of named entities, who are responsible for specific tasks.
- On the last level, we find divine beings who are usually not named but identified by the tasks they perform: Messengers and other divine workers.[4]

ANCIENT ISRAELITE RELIGION.

Let's first look at the similarities between the Ugarit and ancient Israelite religion. The word Asherah occurs about 40 times in the Hebrew Bible, and in most cases it is used as a symbol for a tree or pole, that must be avoided. However, in about six cases it is used as an actual name. Archaeologists continue to make some extraordinary discoveries in these lands. One of particular interest, is a jar with the following picture (artist impression) on it:

---

4   Smith, Mark S. (2001-07-13). The Origins of Biblical Monotheism: Israel's Polytheistic Background and the Ugaritic Texts (Kindle Location 1400). Oxford University Press. Kindle Edition.

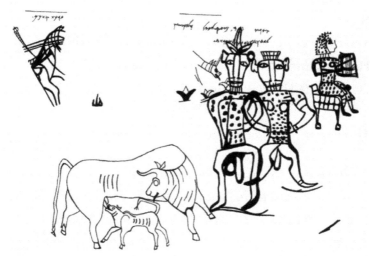

It is the inscription on it that has caused much debate. It pronounces a blessing on a deceased person saying, may this person be blessed *"By Yahweh of Samaria and his Asherah."*

The Biblical writer certainly knew of Asherah. Many scholars think that the pairing of El, with breasts and womb (El Shadday) in Genesis 49:26, is a reference to El's wife. It is not only Asherah that is known by name but a number of monsters and gods. In fact, the earlier the scriptural writings, the more gods are known by name.

Baal, in the Ugaritic text and Yahweh in the Hebrew Bible also shared the same monstrous enemies, namely:

Sea (Hebrew yam, Ugaritic ym, also known by the name, River);

The Biblical Leviathan is the same as the Ugaritic ltn;

Hebrew tannin, Ugaritic tnn or tunnanu;

Death - the Hebrew mawet and Ugaritic Mot.

Three of these ancient enemies are named in Psalm 74:

> *Yet God my King is from of old, working salvation in the midst of the earth. You divided the **sea** by your might; you broke the heads of the **sea monsters (tannin)** on the waters. You crushed the heads of **Leviathan**; you gave him as food for the creatures of the wilderness.*
> (Psalm 74:12–14 ESV)

Ancient Israelite religion had deep roots within the Middle Eastern cultures. They knew the same gods by name. Their religion was built on the same patriarchal family unit as their neighbors. There were home shrines, altars and sacred trees and poles within the family grounds. (See Judges 6) Patriarchs like Abraham and Noah would build altars wherever and whenever the need arose. This practice would later be banished as the need for one central place of worship became more urgent. The people of Israel were often found worshiping other gods and the later prophets would warn against it sternly.

Scholars suggest that premonarchic Israelite religion had a similar hierarchy as Ugarit:

- Level 1: El and Asherah
- Level 2: Baal, Astarte, Shahar, Shalim, Resheph, and Deber Yahweh, the outsider from Edom/Midian/Paran/Seir/Sinai
- Level 3: unknown
- Level 4: Messengers (angels) and servants.[5]

The truth is that early Israelites were very familiar with many of the gods of the region and although later editors tried to hide these ties, many clues remain within the text:

"My father was a wandering Aramean" (Deuteronomy 26:5 HCSB).

Gideon's father worshiped Baal (Judges 6).

The Edomites are called 'your brother' (Deut 23:7).

This early positive relationship with the Edomites, supports the proposal made by a number of theologians[6] that 'Yahweh' has its origins in Edom, as is implied in this verse: *"LORD [Yahweh], when You came from Seir, when You marched from the fields of Edom"* (Judges 5:4 HCSB).

The emergence of Israel's monotheism out of their polytheistic background is probably best described by

5   Mark S. Smith. Memoirs of God (Kindle Locations 1818-1819).
6   Toorn 1996, Lang 2002, Mark S. Smith

this phrase in Genesis 32:28. As Jacob is given the name Israel, he is told: *"for you have striven with gods and men"*.

Elohim (translated god or gods) is plural, but depending on the context it can be interpreted as singular. With our monotheistic glasses we have often translated it as singular. However, in this case the plural gives us a beautiful insight. Israel, with deep roots in the polytheistic cultures of the region, would strive with these views to eventually produce a vision of the one God over all the nations.

EL AND YAHWEH.

We are examining how Israelite monotheism emerged out of the polytheistic region in which they were situated. What I will attempt to show in the next section is that some of the oldest texts within the scriptures were written by authors who held to a polytheistic faith.

The song of Moses in Deuteronomy 32 is considered one of the oldest texts in the Bible. It tells the story of Israel's deliverance from Egypt and it gives us an amazing insight into how Yahweh became Israel's God. In Thom Stark's book, entitled: *The Human Faces of God*, he quotes Deuteronomy 32:8,9 from three different sources as follows:

When Elyon divided the nations,
when he separated the sons of Adam,
he established the borders of the nations

according to the number of the sons of Israel.
Yahweh's portion was his people
Jacob his allotted inheritance.
(MT = Masoretic Text between 800-1000 AC)

When the Most High divided the nations,
when he scattered the sons of Adam,
he established the borders of the nations
according to the number of God's angels,
and his people Jacob became a portion for the Lord,
the land of Israel his inheritance.
(LXX = The Septuagint, the Greek translation of the
Hebrew scriptures, about 2nd century BC)

When Elyon divided the nations,
when he separated the sons of Adam,
he established the borders of the nations
according to the number of the sons of the gods.
Yahweh's portion was his people,
Jacob his allotted inheritance.
(DSS = Dead Sea Scrolls text)

The MT text says he divided the nations according to the
sons of Israel. The LXX says he divided the nations according
to the *number of God's angels.* Why this difference?

In 1947 the Dead Sea Scrolls were discovered. The scrolls
predate the MT text by about a thousand years. It is in

this text that the most original reading is found: The Most High God divided the nations according to the *number of the sons of the gods*. This phrase, *the sons of the gods*, is a typical phrase that occurs in Ugaritic, Akkadian, Aramaic and Phoenician inscriptions and it always refers to second tier deities in the pantheon of gods. What we have here is a classic polytheistic understanding. In Canaanite religion the name of the God at the head of the pantheon is El Elyon. Israel, remember, is part of this region. According to this text the gods have gathered for a council. The most high God, Elyon, is dividing the nations among his sons. Yahweh, one of his sons, is given an inheritance, namely, the nation of Jacob.

Later monotheistic scribes could no longer tolerate such language and so changed the text to reflect their views. The authors of the LXX text and the MT text each found their own unique solution to this problematic polytheistic text.

In verses 41-43, Yahweh is portrayed as an up-and-coming warrior deity who demands the respect of other gods. In verse 43 the DSS reads:

Praise, O heavens, his people
Kneel before him, all you gods.
(4QDeutQ)

Again, these references to other gods were changed in the LXX and MT texts.

The first commandment is another example of polytheism: "*I am the LORD thy God, which have brought thee out of the land of Egypt, out of the house of bondage. Thou shalt have no other gods before me*" (Exodus 20:2–3 KJV).

The text does not say: "I am Yahweh, the only God, you shall have no false gods before me."
No!
It says: "I am Yahweh *your* God."
Why?
Because Yahweh is the one who delivered you from Egypt!
Therefore, don't have any other gods before me!
It continues to state that Yahweh is a jealous God.
Why be jealous if there is no competition?
The first commandment does not deny the existence of other gods but prohibits the worship of other gods because Yahweh is Israel's deliverer.

In Psalm 89 we have another picture of a sacred assembly in which Yahweh is exalted above the other sons of El.

> *LORD[YHVH], the heavens praise Your wonders,*
> *Your faithfulness also,*
> *in the assembly of the holy ones.*

For who in the skies can compare with the LORD[YHVH]?
Who among the heavenly beings[b̄en 'ēl] is like the
LORD[YHVH]?
God is greatly feared in the council of the holy ones,
more awe-inspiring than all who surround Him.
(Psalms 89:5–7 HCSB).

The straightforward translation of "*b̄en 'ēl*" is "sons of el". Who among the sons of El is like YHVH? Again we see a clear picture of YHVH ascending among the gods.

The texts we have discussed are some of the oldest within the Bible and they reveal a polytheistic worldview. How did Israel's monotheism develop? There are many excellent theological resources available on the subject - see the recommended reading list at the back of the book. However, the following is a short overview of the development.

How Yahweh became El

Within tribal-nation communities, the progress of the nation was directly related to the strength of its god as demonstrated by its victories in battle. In many cases a tribe who lost a battle would adopt the god of the victorious tribe.

Israel's boast in Yahweh was directly related to its own ambitions as a nation. See Exodus 15:11-16. As Israel grew in stature and became more powerful, the northern and southern kingdoms uniting under one monarch, it was only natural to also promote Yahweh in their theology.

Yahweh became identified with El, the most high god. In Psalm 82 we see Yahweh, Israel's god, taking the place of the most high god in the council of the gods. He berates the gods of the other nations for not executing justice and then makes this judgment: all the other gods will die.

In this one psalm we not only see the ascension of Yahweh to the position of the supreme EL, we might even have a clue as to how they imagined the most high god became the only living God.

God[elohiym] standeth in the congregation of the mighty[el];
he judgeth among the gods[elohiym].
How long will ye judge unjustly,
and accept the persons of the wicked?
Selah.
Defend the poor and fatherless:
do justice to the afflicted and needy.
Deliver the poor and needy:
rid them out of the hand of the wicked.
They know not, neither will they understand;
they walk on in darkness:
all the foundations of the earth are out of course.
I have said, Ye are gods[elohiym];

and all of you are children of the most High[elyown].
But ye shall die like men,
and fall like one of the princes.
Arise, O God[elohiym], judge the earth:
for thou shalt inherit all nations.
(Psalm 82:1–8 KJV)

Israel's god is no longer a tribal god, whose inheritance is Israel alone. He pronounces the death judgment on all other gods. And so he becomes the judge of all the earth and inherits all the nations.

Israel's theological journey has taken them from a nation with an ambitious second level god, YHVH, to a nation with a position of prominence as YHVH became the most revered among the gods, to a coup in which YHVH took the place of El and put an end to all other gods.

As with all theological journeys, not everyone within a community makes the same journey at the same time. The prohibitions against the worship of 'foreign' gods becomes stronger. The very fact that the worship of foreign gods is condemned is evidence that some still believed in them.

Israel's monotheism comes to a climax during the monarchical period. Having one God gives great impetus to having one central place of worship and consolidating power under one king. Specifically King Josiah introduces strict reforms in which all high places are torn down and all priests who perform rituals outside the officially approved temple in Jerusalem are slaughtered. The prophets who speak during this time, such as Jeremiah, are the first to ridicule the idea of the existence of any other gods. The impact of exile also played a major role in consolidating their theology.

The later hierarchy of Israelite religion was therefore transformed to look like the following:

- Level 1: Yahweh-El
- Level 2: None
- Level 3: "The satan" (Discussed in Chapter 10)
- Level 4: Messengers (angels) and servants.

SUMMARY

We have looked at the influences that have shaped humanity's understanding of God. As such our investigation could only have a very human point of view. A cynical conclusion would be that the whole Israelite religion was a human invention to promote their own national ambitions. On the other hand, many believe that Israel's unique monotheism is the product of nothing less than a divine revelation in which the one true God begins to reveal himself to humanity.

As with all human history, it is probably a bit of both. God enters into conversation with us in the midst of all our confusion and turmoil. We often have glimpses of God and use these moments of inspiration to promote our own selfish ambitions. But He does not abandon us to our confusion - He continues to woo us into relationship, into an understanding that gives life.

And so, the polytheistic worldview of ancient Israelite religion was typical of its region. As we will see in the next chapter on sacrifice, their concepts of violence and the sacred were typical as well. Let me state it as plainly as I know how: Early Israelite religion had its origin, not in a divine revelation, but in the same sacred violence and blindness that birthed all sacrificial religions. It was exactly because they were so typical, that they could become so relevant in transforming these misconceptions of God. And so God entered into a unique conversation with Israel, but one that would be relevant to all nations.

Being aware of the development of ideas throughout the scriptures is essential in grasping the significance of Jesus Christ, who came in the fullness of time (Eph 1:10), to give us understanding (1 John 5:20).

8 - STORY OF SACRIFICE

In chapter five we explored Mimetic Realism which included the processes that lead to the ancient practice of sacrifice. Sacrifice has its origin in prehistoric times, long before the invention of writing. It is therefore not surprising that the scriptures do not pretend to give us a historically accurate account of how or why sacrifice began. It simply assumes that sacrifice was part of human practice since the very beginning, as shown by the story of Cain and Abel. In the previous chapter we saw how Israel was born through a *struggle with gods and men,* how it shared the same polytheistic heritage as its neighbors, but started moving into a whole new direction.

My intention with this chapter is to show that human sacrifices formed part of early Israelite religion. Their conception of the function and value of sacrifice begins just like any other nation but then follows a path of dramatic transformation. The practice of human sacrifice was later condemned as their theology developed. The story of sacrifice in the Hebrew Bible is a dynamic and changing one - we will attempt to trace its path of development.

HUMAN SACRIFICE

As with their neighbors, Israel believed in the power of sacrifice. The more valuable the sacrifice, the more effective it would be. As such, the ultimate sacrifice was human sacrifice. Despite later condemnation of the practice, it is clear that human sacrifice was in fact part of their early history. The recurring theme of a beloved son, given up as dead and then received back, alive again, is found throughout the scriptures. The stories of Abraham, Isaac, Ismael, Jacob and Joseph are some of the more famous examples. These themes are what survived the actual practice of child sacrifice. Let's start with the most basic and most shocking reference to it:

Give Me the firstborn of your sons.
(Exodus 22:29 HCSB)

Many who read this today, spiritualize it. They interpret it as some kind of sacred dedication, but the next verse makes clear what is meant: *"You shall do the same with your oxen and with your sheep: seven days it shall be with its mother; on the eighth day you shall give it to me"* (Ex. 22:30). This clearly refers to the actual practice of sacrifice.

However, provision was made for a substitute sacrifice to be offered: *"All that open the womb are mine, all your male livestock, the firstborn of cow and sheep. The firstborn of a donkey you shall redeem with a lamb, or if you will not redeem it you shall break its neck. All the firstborn of your sons you shall redeem. And none shall appear before me empty-handed"* (Exodus 34:19–20 ESV).

Donkeys were obviously more useful within an agricultural society and so the firstborn of a donkey could be redeemed by the sacrifice of a lamb. Firstborn sons were also more valuable than any animal, and so Israel was commanded to provide a substitute sacrifice.

Some argue that because God made provision for a substitute sacrifice, he therefore never intended to have the firstborn sacrificed. But if the authors thought that God did not desire human sacrifice, why not say that? The clear logic of this command is that Israel's early conceptions of God are that he requires human sacrifice, just as all the other tribal gods of the region. In the same manner as a substitute sacrifice can be offered for a donkey, it can be offered for the firstborn son as well. If no substitute was provided for the donkey, then it had to die. If no substitute was provided for the firstborn son, he had to die. These passages do not forbid human sacrifice, they validate it.

Many other references within the scriptures show that Israel believed in the effectiveness of human sacrifice. One of Israel's kings, Manasseh, sacrificed his own son (2 Kings 21). Obviously these actions were condemned by later authors, but the reason such human sacrifices happened in the first place is because this ancient ritual had deep roots within their consciousness.

In Judges 11:29-40 Jephthah, in the midst of a fierce battle, makes a vow to Yahweh. If Yahweh gives them the victory, he will sacrifice the first one to greet him when he returns home. This is apparently such an appealing deal for Yahweh, that he immediately grants the victory! On Jephthah's return, it is his daughter that is the first one to greet him. He is obviously deeply disturbed, but his daughter says to him: "*My father, you have given your word to the LORD [YHVH]. Do to me as you have said, for the LORD[YHVH] brought vengeance on your enemies...*"

Jephthah does what he promised - he murders his own daughter in honor of Yahweh's great victory. Yahweh does not stop him. Nothing in the text condemns his action. Instead Jephthah is celebrated for his faithfulness even in later Christian Scripture (Heb 11:33-34).

Another instance where child sacrifice is mentioned, is found in Micah 6:

> *With what shall I come before the LORD,*
> *and bow myself before God on high?*
> *Shall I come before him with burnt offerings,*
> *with calves a year old?*
> *Will the LORD be pleased with thousands of rams,*

> *with ten thousands of rivers of oil?*
> *Shall I give my firstborn for my transgression,*
> *the fruit of my body for the sin of my soul?"*
> *He has told you, O man, what is good;*
> *and what does the LORD require of you*
> *but to do justice, and to love kindness,*
> *and to walk humbly with your God?*[1]

As with many of the other prophets, Micah is critical of the sacrificial practice, if the weightier issues of justice and love are neglected. However, the offerings and sacrifices he mentions are all acceptable, and in some cases required by the law. Calves, rams, and oil were all acceptable sacrifices and the sequence in which they are mentioned is one of increasing value:

(1) a year old calf;
(2) thousands of rams;
(3) tens of thousands of rivers of oil;
and the most valuable sacrifice is mentioned last, (4) *"Shall I give my firstborn for my transgression"*

Some would protest and say that this was never the desire or intention of Yahweh and that the very purpose of this text is to show that God values justice and kindness above sacrifice. That is true. But we should also see the tradition and mindset that this text was combating. In fact, in the

---

1   Micah 6:6–8 ESV

case of David, it is exactly his firstborn that Yahweh requires for his transgression of adultery according to the author. He did indeed *give his firstborn for his transgression,* which Micah describes as the most valuable *sacrifice.*

Israel begins with a concept of sacrifice and of God which is as bloody and horrific as any of their neighbor's ideologies. Sacrificial violence remains the same between tribes, despite the differences in ritual. The "sacred" violence of sacrificing one in order to end the profane violence in which many die is seen as redemptive. Violence and warrior-like tribal-gods go hand in hand. Sacrifice and conceptions of gods who delight in bloody violence also go hand in hand. These early perceptions of God were captured in their writings.

THE VIOLENCE OF YAHWEH

It was precisely in rage, violence and war that ancient Israel often saw the holiness, the glory, and the majesty of Yahweh.

Son of man, prophesy and say, Thus says the Lord, say: "A sword, a sword is sharpened and also polished, sharpened for slaughter, polished to flash like lightning! ...

"As for you, son of man, prophesy. Clap your hands and let the sword come down twice, yes, three times, the sword for those to be slain. It is the sword for the great slaughter, which surrounds them, that their hearts may melt, and

many stumble. At all their gates I have given the glittering sword. Ah, it is made like lightning; it is taken up for slaughter."

(Ezekiel 21:9–15 ESV)

Commenting on this passage Raymund Schwager writes:

In this bloody song the sword appears like a personified power rushing to a feast of killing at Yahweh's orders. God seems to harbor a secret pleasure in murder and to become himself so blinded in bloody intoxication that he will wipe out the just together with the guilty. Before the song we read:

"Thus says the LORD: Behold, I am against you and will draw forth my sword out of its sheath, and will cut off from you both righteous and wicked. Because I will cut off from you both righteous and wicked, therefore my sword shall be drawn from its sheath."
(Ezekiel 21:3–4)

God seems to forget himself in his killing. In His bloody orgy he ignores the differences between the guilty and the innocent; at least that is how it sounds in Ezekiel. Similar gruesome texts about Yahweh's actions can be found in the book of Jeremiah:
"Thus says the Lord of hosts:
Behold, evil is coming forth from nation to nation, and a great tempest is stirring from the farthest parts of the earth!

And those slain by the Lord on that day shall extend from one end of the earth to the other."
(Jer 24:32-33)

These are not exceptional events; the judgment is described as a universal occurrence. Those slain by the Lord cover the earth from one end to the other. The universality of the avenging and condemning divine violence parallels the universality of human violence.[2]

These conceptions of an angry and violent Yahweh are not isolated. Neither is the anger always portrayed as just punishment for evil. Rather, God is at times portrayed as one who kills and murders irrationally, even the righteous... because he can and because he wants to.

After events of blind passion and uncontrolled rage, man often employs reason in service of these passions. The gods we project look very much like the sacred violence we initiate and engage in. The stories we tell externalize our conflicts and attempt to give meaning to what is in reality our own self-gratifying, senseless violence.

However, there is a progression in the way Yahweh's violence is perceived. (1)The idea of an irrational murderous God, who slays the guilty and the innocent in uncontrolled rage, slowly makes way for (2)a God who reacts to human evil - a righteously revengeful God. (3)Direct acts of violence are

---

2   Must There Be Scapegoats, Raymund Schwager, page 53

also progressively replaced by images of indirect violence: God handing one nation over into the merciless hands of another. (4)Finally the idea develops that evil returns to the wicked, that violent suffering is the consequence of our actions... that our violence is our own.

SPEAKING OUR BLOODY LANGUAGE

Sacrifice, with all it says about the divine, is yet another concept which God would subvert. He enters into conversation with Israel and makes some very strange declarations through the prophets:

> *Sacrifice and offering thou didst not desire; mine ears hast thou opened: burnt offering and sin offering hast thou not required.*
> (Psalms 40:6 KJV)[3]

The concepts of gods who delight in the blood and flesh of animals, and especially of humans, are starting to be challenged. The most famous child-sacrifice story is of course that of Abraham and Isaac.

> *Take your son," He said, "your only son Isaac, whom you love, go to the land of Moriah, and offer him there as a burnt offering on one of the mountains I will tell you about.*
> (Genesis 22:2 HCSB)

---

3   See also Ps 50:8-15, 51:16, Is 1:11, Jer 6:20, Hos 6:6, Amos 5:21, Mic 6:6.

In a society in which such a request would not be uncommon, Abraham does not question the morality of this request. He does not protest that such a barbaric practice is beneath Yahweh. His concern is more with the promise of an offspring and the fact that Isaac is his only son. However, he obeys.

Let's first be clear that there is nothing in the text that condemns child sacrifice. In fact Abraham is another faith hero because of his willingness to make the greatest sacrifice.

However, I do see this event as a critical point in which God enters into conversation with mankind. He enters into conversation, using the only bloody language we know - the language of sacrifice, and begins to undo our deeply deceptive mythologies of who he is. He stops Abraham moments before he thrusts the knife into his son and provides a substitute sacrifice. Is this the beginning of the end of child sacrifice? Does this mark the beginning of God's self-revelation as a God very different from humanity's projections - a mythological deity who requires blood?

Why would God engage in sacrificial practices if it has such satanic, violent and horrific origins? Again and again he reminds Israel "*Sacrifice and offering I did not desire*". In other words, we were the ones who were so deeply trapped within sacrificial practices and the mythologies they represented that the only way in which he could engage with us was to start where we were at.

CONDEMNATION OF CHILD SACRIFICE

What we do know is that attitudes towards child sacrifice began to change. So much so, that later prophets openly condemned it.

Jeremiah's strategy was to deny that Yahweh ever commanded sacrifice and to state that all such sacrifice was demanded by a different deity, namely Baal.

> *They have built high places to Baal on which to burn their children in the fire as burnt offerings to Baal, something I have never commanded or mentioned; I never entertained the thought.*
> (Jeremiah 19:5 HCSB)

Why was child-sacrifice a practice in Israel, and why would Jeremiah feel compelled to clarify that Yahweh never commanded human sacrifice? Could it be that people knew and practiced the very clear command in Exodus: "*Give Me the firstborn of your sons.*"

> *The threefold denial of the origin of the practice in YHWH's will - 'which I never commanded, never decreed, and which never came into my mind' - suggest that the prophet doth protest too much. Could it be that Jeremiah's hearers saw themselves not as apostates or syncretists but*

as faithful YHWHists following the ancient tradition of their religion? ... the last of the three denials in Jer 19:5 ("which never came into my mind," ...) would be pointless if the author intended to say only that YHWH forbade the rite in question. It appears, instead, that Jeremiah's attack on child sacrifice are aimed not only at the practice itself, but also at the tradition that YHWH desires it.[4]

Ezekiel also needs to explain why Israel used to sacrifice children, and why it is no longer acceptable. Apparently Ezekiel does not think he'll get away with simply denying that Yahweh ever commanded it, and so he presents a very different solution. According to Ezekiel, Israel made Yahweh mad, so mad that he gave them commandments that were 'not good' in order to teach them a lesson.

Wherefore I gave them also statutes that were not good, and judgments whereby they should not live; And I polluted them in their own gifts, in that they caused to pass through the fire all that openeth the womb, that I might make them desolate, to the end that they might know that I am the LORD.
(Ezekiel 20:25–26 KJV)

---

4   The Death and Resurrection of the Beloved Son, by Jon D. Leverson, page 4

Wow! Really!

One prophet denies that Yahweh ever gave these commands. The other explains it as Yahweh being really ticked off and therefore demanding the life of the firstborn, "*all that open the womb*", so that he may desolate them!

So which one is true?

Both these prophets had to reinterpret past religious practices that were no longer acceptable. They are in the midst of a changing conversation, and at times an embarrassing conversation. Maybe Jeremiah is a bit closer to the truth when he says that such practices were never God's idea, but to deny that it is part of Israel's history with Yahweh won't work.

Ezekiel's explanation simply maintains the mythological picture of an angry God. His view of sacrifice is changing, but he still holds to his view of a violent God.

Paul said we should not be surprised if Satan comes disguised as an angel of light. Similarly, we should not be surprised if the most basic religious practice is a mask for the most evil deed. Sacrifice became the religiously approved means of murder.

No wonder Jesus says in Matthew 11:27 *No one knows the Father except the Son.*

SUMMARY

The true horror of perverted desire, the conflict and violence it gives birth to, the satanic sacrificial system that results from it, and the twisted ideas about God that originate in it, are starting to be exposed. The full exposure would only come in Christ as he would take us back to the actual event that skewed our ideas of God... skewed ideas that are just as prevalent in much of Christianity today as in any other man-made religion.

God enters our conversation as demonstrated in the history of Israel, slowly starting to undo our concepts. This discourse is the necessary beginning. The collective self-deception within religious communities could ultimately not be broken by any amount of discourse alone. It therefore took the real act of Jesus' life, death and resurrection to bring us face to face with the formative events of our past and thereby overturn the deceitfulness of language.

9 - Paradox of Evil

What is evil?

Answers to this question have often been very abstract and theoretical. In reality, though, we encounter evil not as some abstract theory but as a very real experience.

Stubbing one's toe might cause some pain, some suffering, but we are unlikely to label it as evil for two reasons. Firstly, the significance of the event and the consequent suffering is too small. Secondly, there was no evil intent. It was simply an accident. Not all suffering is evil.

Now if someone specifically places a brick in a dark hallway for the purpose of inflicting pain, that comes closer to being described as evil because there was actual intent to harm. The significance of a stubbed toe, though, is probably still too small to label as evil.

The size of the harm caused, influences our perceptions. The tsunami of 2010 was a natural disaster. There was no evil intent present when the tectonic plates of the earth moved and indirectly caused the deaths of more than 200,000 people. However, the size of the disaster was so overwhelming that it is easy to perceive it as evil, especially if you lost loved ones as a result.

The most acute experience of evil is where the intensity and duration of suffering coincides with deliberate intent to cause harm. So we can say that not all suffering is evil, but all evil is experienced as suffering.

Nowhere is the experience of evil more intense than in the event of the founding murder. The victim's mutilated corpse is where humanity first becomes aware of its own violence … of its own evil. However, we humans are not that good at recognizing and dealing with evil within ourselves, but we are rather talented at projecting and externalizing our fears.

Unwilling to recognize ourselves as the source of our victims' suffering, we ask ourselves where the suffering comes from? What has defiled this victim so as to attract this kind of retribution from a faceless justice? The language of defilement and retribution becomes one of the earliest ways in which humans describe how order is restored to a chaotic world. Because defilement attracts vengeance, laws that prohibit defilement as well as purification rites to cleanse defilement come into being.

All suffering became associated with punishment for defilement. If a person got sick, had relational problems, or happened upon some misfortune, the immediate question raised was: What did I do to attract this? What defilement, what sin caused this suffering?

And so, mistakenly, the evil of suffering becomes synonymous with the evil of sin. Ethics become mixed up with the physics of suffering. Paul Ricoeur writes:

> *Two indications in the experience of evil point towards this underlying unity of the human condition. On the side of moral evil, the first experience of guilt entails, as its dark side, the feeling of having been seduced by overwhelming powers and, consequently, our feeling of belonging to a history of evil, which is always already there for everyone. This strange experience of passivity, at the heart of evildoing, makes us feel ourselves to be victims in the very act that makes us guilty. This same blurring of the boundaries between guilt and being a victim can also be observed if we start from the other pole. Since punishment is a form of suffering allegedly deserved, who knows whether all suffering is not in one way or another the punishment for some personal or collective fault, either known or unknown? It is this dark background of both guilt and suffering that makes evil such a unique enigma.[1]*

To summarize, the human condition is one in which we have all encountered evil, both as suffering victims and guilty participants. Mimetic theory, addressing psychological,

---

1   Paul Ricoeur. Figuring the Sacred: Religion, Narrative and Imagination (Kindle Locations 3696-3701). Kindle Edition.

anthropological and sociological dimensions of our existence, goes a long way in explaining moral evil. As far as twisted mimetic desire is concerned, we are all both victims of the societies we reflect and guilty participants in a society that causes harm. Evil is intrinsically part of the perverted mimetic cycle.

EARLY STORIES

The myths, inspired by the founding murder, also gave birth to tribal gods that embody our evils and personify our fear of vengeance and suffering. And so gods who delight in violence and blood were created in the image and likeness of man.

Evil, remember, is for the most part experienced not as an abstract theory but as something very concrete that always involves some form of suffering. Language is the collection of symbols we use with which to describe these events and experiences. The actual events pass away and memories fade; and so our stories become more and more important for they alone remain. Over time our symbols can take on a life of their own. Successive generations might not experience the same suffering that birthed these stories, but the legends and personification of evil will continue to haunt them.

The oldest recorded stories dealt with these experiences of suffering, especially with the reality of death. Death often came early, uninvited and violently. Even in the few cases where people lived a full life, death remained the most difficult fact to deal with. Coming face to face with our own mortality is an experience that asks the most disturbing questions of us:

Is this the end?

Was my life worth anything?

Do I have meaning?

Does anything have lasting meaning?

Why do we suffer?

Why do we die, and why is violence so prevalent in our world?

These are the questions our myths tried to address. According to René Girard it is the very event of the founding murder that is at the heart of many of these myths.

In Enuma Elish, mankind is created at the end of a brutal battle from nothing less than the blood of Kingu, a war-commander god. The message is clear. We began in violence. It is part of what makes us human. Many other origin myths include violence in their accounts of the formation of mankind.

ESCALATING VIOLENCE

As we have already seen, the Biblical testimony also points to violence as the most obvious expression of evil. The first social sin is the violent murder of Abel. Cain, the murderer, then establishes the city of the Canaanites. The first civilization is born from a violent situation. In order to deter anyone from murdering Cain, a new law is introduced. If anyone murders Cain, he will be avenged seven times. The imagined solution to murder is multiple murders! The imagined solution to violence is greater violence! Escalating violence seems inevitable. The story of Noah tells of a world so full of violence that God simply wants to get rid of it.

Have you noticed that in all this talk about evil, suffering and violence, that these early stories do not identify a personality called Satan as the cause of evil? In fact early Hebrew writings know very little about the figure Christians are so familiar with today. Violence is seen as the number one manifestation of evil and cause of suffering. This evil would eventually be personified, but that transition takes place over many generations and in different iterations of stories. Let's follow these transitions.

TRANSFORMATION OF EVIL FROM POLYTHEISM TO MONOTHEISM

Ancient Israelite religion began within a society that had a polytheistic worldview. Within such a worldview, the problem of evil is partly abstracted into a conflict between the gods. There are many gods who have different interests and purposes. No one god is supreme and they compete, sometimes violently, to have their will done.

Tribes have a mutually beneficial relationship with the tribal god they revere. The tribe provides the deity with sacrifices and such honors, while the god gives them victories in war and shows favor in other ways such as good weather, harvests, etc.

The suffering a tribe experiences is therefore either caused by another stronger deity or by offending the tribal deity. For the most part the local tribal god is good to us and foreign gods want to harm us. In other words, some evil is caused by powers greater than the local god and therefore nothing can be done about it, or alternatively, the local god is causing the suffering because the tribe offended him in some way.

Moving from a polytheistic worldview to a monotheistic worldview changes all of this. When there is only one God whose will is absolute and whose power is all-encompassing, the problem of evil becomes much more acute. In such early monotheistic theories God is the source of all things, including evil.

And so we read passages that argue this exact point:

> *I am the LORD, and there is none else. I form the light, and create darkness: I make peace, and create evil: I the LORD do all these things.*
> (Isaiah 45:6–7 KJV)

There is a thread of theological thought in the scriptures that assigns everything - good and evil, peace and war, suffering and deliverance - to the one God from whom are all things. This however has serious consequences for one's understanding of the nature and character of God. It was just as uncomfortable then as it is now to explain to a person why their child was born with a deformity, or why their teenage son died a violent death, or why they will soon be dead due to an incurable sickness... and simultaneously maintain that God is good and just and means them no harm.

Job must be one of the earliest protesters. He argues that his suffering is undeserved, unjust and cannot be explained by the usual human reasoning. These voices of lament increase in intensity throughout the scriptures. Against our most eloquent arguments and theologies of God's sovereignty and justice these voices maintain that they are innocent, yet they suffer. These delicate theories eventually need to face the harsh reality of human experience.

And so early forms of monotheism paint a picture of God which is as beautiful and as ugly as the realities of life. Such a God is as much involved in murder as he is in the birthing of a new life. Natural disasters that indiscriminately take the lives of thousands are as much under his direct control as the blooming of a flower. This God causes as much suffering as he causes joy; he is as evil as he is good. Although the adherents would not use such words, the conclusion is clear.

So within this early Israelite monotheistic theology, pressures mount to explain the reality of the suffering we experience and the supposed goodness and sovereignty of God.

SUMMARY

Mankind's struggle with evil did not begin as a supernatural battle against an evil spiritual being. It was the very real struggle with violence, death, suffering, fear and guilt that inspired our stories. Often mankind stood helpless against natural forces or against the communal influences that forced us to act in a certain way. Reverting to language, to elaborate stories, was often the only way in which we could still have a say in what seemed inevitable. Our myths and philosophies were the only way in which to purge ourselves of the unbearable guilt. However, being so deeply involved and invested in the processes that secured our communities, we remained blind to the fact that we were the cause of much suffering.

Inevitably, God became implicated in many of our stories. The very nature of God is at risk in the way we explain evil. Consequently our understanding of evil hugely influenced our theologies of who and what God is.

In the next chapter, *History of Satan*, we'll look at the one particularly popular idea that developed in response to the paradox of evil.

10 - HISTORY OF SATAN

The story of Satan has a history and a progression that can be followed throughout scripture. It is a story which attempts to deal with the paradox of evil and, as we will see, it has many branches and interpretations.

In the Hebrew Bible or Old Testament, *the satan* features very seldom and the creature that Christianity is familiar with as Satan, never features. We have read back later ideas into these stories to find him there. But if we allow these stories to speak within their own cultural historic context, we will find that our contemporary and well-known figure of Satan is not a character they knew anything about. Let's see how their ideas of evil and the satan developed.

SATAN - THE VERY DOWN-TO-EARTH ENEMY
The Hebrew word 'satan' is not a name but a noun. As such it is often used with the definite article as in "*the*" *accuser*, "*the*" *adversary*, "*the*" *stumbling block*. Earthly enemies are described as the satan on numerous occasions.

*Send that man back and let him return to the place you assigned him. He must not go down with us into battle only to become **our adversary** during the battle.*

(1 Samuel 29:4 HCSB)

*David answered, "Sons of Zeruiah, do we agree on anything? Have you become **my adversary** today?"*

(2 Samuel 19:22 HCSB)

*So the LORD raised up Hadad the Edomite as **an enemy** against Solomon. He was of the royal family in Edom.*

(1 Kings 11:14 HCSB)

*In return for my love they **accuse** me.*

(Psalms 109:4 HCSB)

All the highlighted words above were translated from the Hebrew word for *satan*.

MONOTHEISM AND SATAN

Over time these earthly enemies, stumbling blocks and accusers began to take on more supernatural qualities within the Hebrew scriptures. The concept of an angel specifically assigned to oppose, accuse and generally act as a prosecuting attorney became a popular image. It is easy to see why. The discomfort within early monotheism, in which God was directly and equally responsible for good and evil, continued to increase. Angelic beings responsible for all the unpleasantness became a theological instrument with which to transfer evil attributes from God onto these subordinates. Conveniently, God remained sovereign, preserving their monotheistic dogma but He was no longer directly responsible for evil. The blame now fell on the prosecuting angel/angels.

> *It is clear that the shift from many gods to a singular Lord of the Universe gives rise to an existential frustration amongst God's chosen people as they grapple with the reality of a God who creates both weal and woe. It would appear that, over time, an exorcism of sorts takes place; the negative aspects of Yhvh are cast out and assigned to alternative beings, such as the Destroyer (Mashit), the 'smiting angel' (hammal'ak kammashit), and of course, hassatan. Eventually it is hassatan, 'the Adversary', who will become the embodiment of evil, but this, too, is a slow, evolutionary process, with many more twists and turns to explore.*[1]

The task of opposing, accusing and prosecuting became associated with one angel in particular. This angel eventually became known as Satan, taking his name from the noun that described his function.

To demonstrate the development of the concept of Satan in early monotheism, we'll examine two versions of a story that describes the same event. One is recorded in 2 Samuel 24, which is the earlier version. The later version is recorded in 1 Chronicles 21.

---

1   T.J. Wray and Gregory Mobley, *The Birth of Satan*, page 51

The basic events of the story, with which both versions correspond, are as follows: David decides to do a census of Israel and Judah. Not everyone agrees with this - it had potential tax implication! Consequently, some debate follows. However, David's decision stands. It takes about nine months to complete the census. Shortly after the census some kind of plague strikes Israel and seventy thousand people die. It is obvious to the writers that David sinned and so caused this just punishment to come upon the nation.

From a purely monotheistic point of view, everything happens under God's control and so 2 Sam 24:1 reads as follows: "*And again the anger of the LORD was kindled against Israel, and he moved David against them to say, Go, number Israel and Judah.*"(2 Samuel 24:1 KJV)

In other words, it is perceived that God is angry with Israel, mad enough to kill seventy thousand of them... but it seems that even YHVH himself does not feel that he has enough justification for such a killing spree and so he devises a plan: he seduces David to do a census and in doing so secures all the justification he needs to carry out his murderous plan.

It is none other that YHVH himself that inspires David to do the census. (the word translated 'moved' can also be translated 'seduced') And it is YHVH himself who sends the plague. This interpretation of the events is in perfect harmony with early monotheism - God is in direct control of everything.

By the time the Chronicler writes his version of the events, the concept of Satan is much further developed and so he interprets the events as follows: "*And Satan stood up against Israel, and provoked David to number Israel.*" (1 Chronicles 21:1 KJV)

Describing the exact same event, the Chronicler can no longer ascribe the evil of the event to God directly. The concept of Satan has developed to the stage where such evil events are no longer directly caused by God but by the accuser, the adversary.

SATAN IN THE HEAVENLY COUNCIL

It's important to note that early references to Satan as a supernatural being do not position him as an adversary to God... not at all. Satan is first portrayed as an obedient servant doing the will of God and in effect relieving God of many unpleasant tasks. Satan is portrayed a number of times as part of the divine council.[2] Again the story of Job illustrates this understanding.

Within these early developments of the concept of Satan he is not perceived as a rebel but rather as a faithful employee. As such he fulfills a vital theological function, namely, he relieves God from direct responsibility for suffering. This

---

2   Zec 3, Job

provided much needed relief within the strict monotheistic framework, but it could not last very long. Is there really much difference between God doing evil and God allowing evil? Theological tensions continued to increase particularly when suffering intensified and when such suffering became personal.

SATAN ACQUIRES AMBITION

So far we have seen how the concept of the satan developed from the natural opposition and enmity people faced, to a supernatural being under God's control, functioning as the prosecutor within the heavenly courts. The next development does not take place until Israel's exile into Babylon (modern day Iraq). It is here that the idea of full scale hostility between God and Satan, light and darkness, good and evil, begins to take shape.

Within Israel's new home Babylon, a radical new religious idea became widely popular. Although it was radical for the Middle East during that time, it was remarkably similar to many later Jewish and Christian ideas. Zoroastrianism was a religion that acknowledged only one true God. Its ideas of evil, the personification of evil, and an afterlife were however much further developed than Israel's ideas.

Zarathustra, the founder of Zoroastrianism, taught that evil did not come from God, directly or indirectly. A separate being called Ahriman was the source of all evil and was in constant battle with the one good God, Ahura Mazda (Wise Lord). In this very moralistic religion, every person had to choose which side of the battle they wanted to fight for. The concepts of final judgment and the afterlife were also well developed within this faith.

It is significant that before Israel's contact with Zoroastrianism, their concepts of resurrection, an afterlife, postmortem judgment and a separate evil being were not developed at all. Only after this contact do we have Jewish writings, such as the book of Enoch, that speculates about the rebellion of the angelic prosecutor, Satan. The ideas proposed in such extra biblical books caught the imagination of some Jewish thinkers (especially a group known as the Pharisees). And as is often the case, these new ideas were then read back into scripture, even though the original authors never even knew of their existence.

These authors are very imaginative and draw on two or three obscure passages from the Hebrew Bible and elaborate them into cosmic sized dramas. (The only authors that have succeeded in being even more imaginative have been our modern Christian fiction writers!) The dramatic imagery, the addictive nature of fear, the opportunity to once again indulge in superstition, make this kind of fiction an instant hit!

By the time Jesus appeared on the scene, these ideas were widely known and had many adherents. But as we will discover in later chapters, Jesus would be exposing the true structure of evil in a way it has never been exposed before.

SUMMARY

The previous few chapters have considered the development of ideas throughout the Hebrew scriptures. This chapter has specifically traced the development of the idea of *Satan*.

What we have explored is far from comprehensive... we have to wait and see what Jesus reveals before we can bring this topic to a conclusion. But before we get there, we have one last developing idea to consider and that is how the expectation for a Messiah began and expanded.

11 - Coming Messiah

The stories of ancient Israel and Judah did not fall out of the sky, they developed during their journeys and so are intricately linked to their history.

Most writings during this time in the Middle East were done by privileged scribes for ruling empires and their official religious institutions. Although such writings could span many topics, their point of view was rather limited. They were almost exclusively written from the perspective of the privileged few, the victors and the rulers.

One aspect that makes the Hebrew narratives so unique is the event that defined them as a nation - the exodus. Deliverance from slavery, the overthrow of the established order, and justice for the oppressed - these were the events that would birth their stories. Although it is true that the scriptures were also produced by the privileged scribal class, their history of oppression and deliverance played an important role in their perspective. Even when they became a free nation these memories would remain definitive in how they understood the world and themselves.

THE EXPECTATION FOR DELIVERANCE

In a polytheistic world where tribal gods were continually vying for position, engaging in tribal warfare was a way of establishing who the strongest god was. It was not uncommon for a tribe who lost a battle to abandon their tribal god and adopt the god of the conquerors. And so many gods perished as their tribes were conquered and assimilated into new tribal communities.

Israel's movement away from a polytheistic worldview into monotheism was an essential key to the survival of their religion even during great defeats. If there was only one God who orchestrated all events then defeat in battle could no longer be seen as a defeat of Yahweh; rather it was interpreted as Yahweh's punishment for their unfaithfulness. This understanding meant that their faith and hope in God could remain alive even during exile, for the God who orchestrates all of history could deliver just as surely as He could discipline.

MESSIANIC HOPE AND THE MONARCHY

Israel's hope for deliverance slowly but surely developed into a hope for a specific kind of deliverer. The establishment of the monarchy did more to shape this expectation than any other influence. The messianic hope began as a political hope.

For many generations the tribes of Judah and Israel were guided and ruled by charismatic judges and prophets. Whenever the need arose for strong leadership, the '*Ruach*' (spirit) of God would come upon such a leader and inspire him or her to accomplish God's will in these tribal communities. This was a type of direct theistic rule through inspired charismatic leaders.

The establishment of the monarchy was therefore not without controversy. In fact the story in 1 Samuel 8 makes it plain that some thought of the monarchy as a rejection of God's rule. The people came and asked Samuel for a "*king to judge us the same as all the other nations have*" (v5). After Samuel spoke to God about this request, Yahweh answers: "*they have not rejected you; they have rejected Me as king*" (v7). A stern warning follows regarding the implications of having a king. A king needs to build and defend his kingdom: labor, taxes and war is an inevitable part of the monarchy. Despite this warning, the people still chose to have a king.

The first king, Saul, is therefore given as a kind of punishment for their insistence on having a king. It is only the second king, David, who is truly anointed of God.

Now we must remember where these people came from. What event defined them? It was Yahweh who heard their cry, who delivered them from Egypt and brought them out of the land of slavery. They remember the violent oppression they suffered; they understand the injustice of empires.

From the very inception of Israel's monarchy, their history demands a very different expectation of both the king and the kingdom. They expect more than a system of oppression, more than war and violence, because they are a people who worship a God who is concerned for the oppressed. They expect a king and a kingdom in which righteousness and justice will reign. Although they moved away from a direct theocratic rule, they still expect God to rule through the mediation of the monarchy. And so the king is declared to be the 'son of God' (Ps 2:7, 89:27) who rules on behalf of God.

These growing expectations of a divine-king are expressed so clearly in Psalm 72:

Give the king your justice, O God,
and your righteousness to your royal son!
May he judge your people with righteousness,
and your poor with justice! ...
May he defend the cause of the poor of my people,
give deliverance to the children of the needy,
and crush the oppressor!
May they fear you while the sun endures,
and as long as the moon, throughout all generations!

May he be like the rain that falls on the mown grass,
like showers that waters the earth!
In his day may the righteous flourish,
and peace abound, till the moon be no more!
May he have dominion from sea to sea,
and from the river to the ends of the earth!
...
may all kings fall down before him,
all nations serve him!
For he delivers the needy when he calls,
the poor and him who has no helper.
He has pity on weak and the needy,
and saves the lives of the needy.
From oppression and violence he redeems their life,
and precious is their blood in his sight.
...
Blessed be the Lord (Yahweh), the God (Elohim) of Israel,
who alone does wondrous things.
Blessed be his glorious name forever;
may the whole earth be filled with His glory!
Amen and Amen!

The name and character of Yahweh defines the kind of king Israel anticipates. The history of Israel's kings, however, is a history of their failure to live up to these expectations. But the kings' failures did not diminish this hope. On the contrary, it served to intensify and transform this hope into something much greater.

David succeeded in securing the borders of Israel, but in many ways he also failed to live up to being the representative of Yahweh.

Then came Solomon the son of David. He is given even greater success and blessed with wisdom and wealth. The kingdom grows during his rule. During this time of peace and prosperity, Solomon decides to build a temple for the Lord. In 1 Kings 5, we read how Solomon drafted "forced labor" of 30,000 laborers, 70,000 burden bearers and 80,000 stonecutters. Forced labor is just another way of saying *slavery*. So in honor of the God who delivers slaves and heeds the cry of the oppressed, Solomon builds a temple using slave labor.

The memory of the God who delivered them from the chariots and horsemen of Egypt begins to grow dim as they are faced with the reality of a prosperous kingdom that needs protection. *"Solomon also had 40,000 stalls of horses for his chariots, and 12,000 horsemen."* (1 Kings 4:26). Later on we read that the import and export of chariots and horses became a major part of the kingdoms prosperity. And so the God who delivered Israel from the violence of the Egyptian empire is now represented by a king and a kingdom that builds Yahweh's temple using slave labor

and generates their wealth through the trade of weapons.
Israel became what they were delivered from.

EXILE AND THE TRANSFORMATION OF EXPECTATION

*So it was not merely the all-too-human failure of the kings
to meet the claim of the divine unction which led to the
messianic hope. It was the constitution of a monarchy that
was set up to save, in the name of the compassionate God.
In the arena of power politics, kingship in the name of the
God who promises mercy can hardly be implemented.
Any such monarchy must by its very nature lead to a hope
which reaches out beyond all experienced political reality,
and which no political reality can ever satisfy. Yet for all
that, this hope remains realistic, for what it expects is not
a religious redeemer of souls, but the 'theopolitical messiah'
(Buber's phrase) of people and country.*

*Under the onslaught of the Assyrian armies, Israel's brief
political independence ended. Her kings were too weak,
too corrupt, and too incapable to stand up to the great
Assyrian power. Yet, 'whereas everywhere else in Syria the
royal ideologies behind the state structures disappeared
with the coming of the Assyrian hegemony, in Israel the
image of the king actually acquired new depths: it was
transformed into the image of the messiah.* [1]

---

1   Jurgen Moltmann, The Way of Jesus Christ, Loc 250, Kindle
version

The destruction of their kingdom and exile into foreign countries awakened their memory of the delivering God once again. It became clear that the way in which they did "kingdom", up until then, was not the kingdom of Yahweh.

During the Assyrian war King Ahaz from the house of David, while busy losing the battle, is given a sign:

> *Behold a young woman will conceive and bear a son, and he will be named Immanuel ... for behold this child knows to refuse evil and choose the good.*
> (Isaiah 7:14-16)

The promise of a deliverer who could live up to the expectations of being a representative of God grew even stronger as the weaknesses and failures of their kings became obvious. This Messianic king would usher in a kingdom unlike any other for "*with righteousness shall he judge the poor, and decide with equity for the meek of the earth...*" (Isaiah 11:4)

This hope is not only intensified during this period of suffering, it is also expanded. For if justice and deliverance from oppression is Yahweh's concern, then Israel's prosperity alone cannot be the goal of His kingdom. No, this will be a kingdom that covers the earth as the waters cover the sea. It will be nothing less than a whole new creation in which violence will forever be vanquished (verses 5-9).

Instead of the all too familiar warrior kings, who grew and protected their kingdoms through violence and oppression, Zechariah has a vision of an entirely different kind of coming king. This king will be humble, put an end to chariots and war horses, and bring peace to all the nations:

> *Behold your king is coming to you;*
> *righteous and salvation is he,*
> *humble and mounted on a donkey,*
> *on a colt, the foal of a donkey.*
> *I will cut off the chariot from Ephraim*
> *and the war horses from Jerusalem;*
> *and the battle bow shall be cut off,*
> *and he shall speak peace to the nations;*
> *his rule shall be from sea to sea,*
> *and from the ends of the river to the ends of the earth.*
> *... return to your stronghold, O PRISONERS OF HOPE.*
> (Zech 9:9-12)

Son of Man

So Israel's expectation for a messiah-king grows, expands and changes their vision of the future. Both the person of this messiah and the nature of his rule undergo radical transformations.

As the people of Israel find themselves in exile, without a king and in need of deliverance, the memory of the servant-prophet Moses again becomes central to the image of this deliverer. It is also during this time that the prophets and priests are with the people - the king is not. It's the prophets and priests that suffer with the community and that keeps the hope for deliverance alive. The portrayal of the expected Messiah therefore takes on a more complex form that includes the image of a suffering servant as a representative of the people rather than an exclusive vision of a victorious king. Many of these suffering-servant passages would be quoted by Jesus in relation to his own self-understanding.

The scope and extent of the expected deliverance grows into a kingdom that encompasses all nations. It is also during an exile that Daniel has a vision of one like the 'son of man' who would bring the history of human empires to an end and break through into our realm with the government of God (Daniel 7).

In this vision, he stands at the end of history and looks back at the empires that have come and gone. Israel does not even feature among them, for in the greater context of human history Israel only played a small part. This vision takes Daniel far beyond the hope of a restored Israel to the hope of a restored humanity: "*there came one like a son of man and he came to the Ancient of Days and was presented before him. And to him was given dominion and glory and a kingdom, that all peoples, nations and languages should serve him; his dominion is an everlasting dominion, which shall not pass away, and his kingdom one that shall not pass away."* [2]

In this vision, the Jewish messiah is also the universal hope of mankind. As the coming Messiah he would deliver Israel; as the son of man he would deliver mankind from a world of perpetual violence into a world of unending peace.

SUMMARY

We have looked at the development of Israel's expectation for a messiah. It was not in the comfort of the philosophers court that these expectations grew, neither were these ideas birthed by supernatural revelation in ultra-spiritual environments. It was in the midst of losing battles, in the depth of real suffering, in the moments of paralyzing disappointment, that the hope for a deliverer was awakened and given shape.

The reality of a never ending cycle of the oppressed becoming the oppressors, of victims becoming the perpetrators of violence and the elite becoming slaves, of kings failing to be just and kingdoms failing to provide freedom, that a new vision arose for a world truly free and truly just. To enter such a new world there would have to be a leader that could transform the deeply entrenched ideas of this world and introduce us to the kingdom of God.

---

2   Daniel 7: 13,14

PART 3 - REDEFINED

12 - History Summarized in His Story

In the previous chapters we considered how our narratives developed: to make sense of our mimetic history, to describe the mystery of God, to lament the paradox of evil, to offer some sort of explanation through the story of Satan, to justify our barbaric sacrificial systems, and to express our hope that somehow all these stories will find a meaningful end. It is in the context and chaos of all these stories that Jesus is born in what Paul describes as the *fullness of time*[1].

Summarizing the Human Story

I will utter things kept secret from the foundation of the world.

(Matthew 13:35 Mounce)

Jesus' story summarizes the human story and offers a conclusion that we were unable to reach ourselves. The circular events in which chaos gives way to order and order succumbs to chaos, the never ending cycle of victors and victims would finally be interrupted by a truly new event.

---

1   Ephesians 1:10

Jesus is the embodiment of a message, the creative word that confronts the meaningless chaos of our own stories. Time would be compressed and the futility of its rivalistic activity would be revealed; simultaneously a new time of true meaning would come about in the self-giving love of this man Jesus Christ.

The whole setting of his story is a micro-cast of the human drama, of our conflicted history. Israel once again finds herself in subjection to a pagan empire - the Roman Empire. Within the Jewish nation there are many factions and competing voices. In the midst of the frustration, the desire for deliverance intensifies. Many would-be messiahs have raised their voices in the thick of these tensions and incited the crowds. Most of them met a violent end. The gospels all seem to race towards the last week of Jesus' life and death. Multiple conflicts, plots and schemes converge in this last week in which all these frustrations fuse and become focused on one.

It is in this chaotic environment that Jesus' teaching and actions are starting to make people nervous. Many who have had their hopes shattered by previous messianic pretenders cannot but whisper of the renewed hope that he is indeed the Messiah. The religious authorities have also noticed him and are increasingly offended at his teachings and popularity. He constantly steps beyond the accepted boundaries, embracing outcasts and thus blurring the social differences. All these events are racing towards the Passover feast when Jews from all over the region would flock to Jerusalem. All the elements for conflict are present: national tensions, religious zeal and personal frustrations. Individuals, families and nations seem to be obliviously swept along currents of conflict. That which we have been unaware of, the unconscious processes upon which we have build our identities and founded our communities - the realities we tried to hide with our myths - that is what Jesus comes to make us conscious of.

BLIND FROM THE BEGINNING.

In John 9 we have a story that begins with an outcast, a blind man who receives his sight, and ends with a group that insists that they can see but are exposed as being blind.

Throughout this story we are drawn back to the very beginning, the very origin of human blindness. A number of phrases point to this formative event in our primal past:

First, the man is **born blind** (9:1).
Second, Jesus spitting on the ground and making mud is a picture of the **Genesis creation story** when God formed man from the earth. Further, the word **mud is used as a pun for Adam** - who derived his name from adamah, the Hebrew word for mud. Again we are reminded of the beginning, the birth of humanity (9:3-7).

Finally, the man testifies of his healing with these words: "*Not **since time began** has it been heard that anyone opened the eyes of a man born blind*" (John 9:32 Mounce).

> *As He was passing by, He saw a man blind from birth. His disciples questioned Him: "As he passed by, he saw a man blind from birth. And his disciples asked him, "Rabbi, who sinned, this man or his parents, that he was born blind?"* (John 9:1–2 ESV)

The disciples' question is revealing: What sin caused this man to suffer and be excluded from full participation in human community? They understand sin as something committed by this man, or his parents, which resulted in his condition. Jesus responds to the question and to the man's condition not with a theoretical explanation but by spitting on the ground, making mud, smearing it on his eyes, and telling him to go wash. "*So he went and washed and came back seeing.*" This causes great commotion in the community as he starts to testify about this extraordinary miracle. He is eventually brought to the council of the pharisees for questioning.

Not hearing what they want to hear, they summon his parents to further answer their questions: "*His parents answered, 'We know that this is our son and that he was born blind. But how he now sees we do not know, nor do we know who opened his eyes. Ask him; he is of age. He will speak for himself.* *(His parents said these things because they feared the Jews, for the Jews had already agreed that if anyone should confess Jesus to be Christ, he was to be put out of the synagogue.)*" (John 9:20–22 ESV)

What is becoming obvious is that many people were deeply touched by Jesus and inwardly believed in him, but there was another power that kept them from openly acknowledging him. This is made plain on a number of other occasions[2] This social power is a contagious mimetic cycle that intimidates and threatens people. In a world of deception and illusion, the fear of exclusion keeps people bound in its own cycle. It is this secret power that Jesus is in the process of exposing.

The blind man, however, is no stranger to exclusion. It seems to have made of him a very honest and courageous man for he is not afraid of speaking the truth even to those who have the power to exclude him.

So for the second time they called the man who had been blind and said to him, "Give glory to God. We know that this man is a sinner." He answered, "Whether he is a sinner I do not know. One thing I do know, that though I was blind, now I see." They said to him, "What did he do to you? How did he open your eyes?" He answered them, "I have told you already, and you would not listen. Why do

---

2   Jonn 12:37,42

you want to hear it again? Do you also want to become his disciples?" And they reviled him, saying, "You are his disciple, but we are disciples of Moses. We know that God has spoken to Moses, but as for this man, we do not know where he comes from." The man answered, "Why, this is an amazing thing! You do not know where he comes from, and yet he opened my eyes. We know that God does not listen to sinners, but if anyone is a worshiper of God and does his will, God listens to him. Never since the world began has it been heard that anyone opened the eyes of a man born blind. If this man were not from God, he could do nothing." They answered him, "You were born in utter sin, and would you teach us?" And they cast him out. (John 9:24–34 ESV)

The first time this man encountered Jesus he was a blind outcast. Now, for the second time, he will meet Jesus again as an outcast. From this and many other similar stories, it seems that the only context in which we meet Jesus and recognize him for who he truly is, is among the outcasts.

Jesus heard that they had cast him out, and having found him he said, "Do you believe in the Son of Man?" He answered, "And who is he, sir, that I may believe in him?" Jesus said to him, "You have seen him, and it is he who is speaking to you." He said, "Lord, I believe," and he worshiped him. Jesus said, "For judgment I came into this world, that those who do not see may see, and those who see may become blind." Some of the Pharisees near him heard these things, and said to him, "Are we also blind?" Jesus said to them, "If you were blind, you would have no guilt; but now that you say, 'We see,' your guilt remains." (John 9:35–41 ESV)

So many assumptions are overturned in this story. The very definition of sin, blindness and exclusion are inverted.

The story began with the assumption that an act of sin caused this man to be blind and excluded; it ends with the revelation that the blindness that causes us to exclude is our sin. Sin has been radically redefined. Sin is exposed as the blind act of exclusion itself. It is by the very act of judging, expelling and of casting out, by which these leaders who claim to see so clearly have judged themselves and exposed their own blindness.

It reveals that the very social and religious systems of manipulation that force people into conformity is the power of this blindness. These are the principalities and powers - the structures we have created to mirror our own perversion. It is only those courageous enough to be outcasts from such systems that have any opportunity to see. Jesus is busy unraveling the twisted mimetic cycle and exposing the very structure of evil.

EXPOSING OUR MODELS

Jesus was keenly aware of the human reflective nature and purposely looked beyond his community to find a true model. In the midst of all these natural influences he refused to simply be a reflection of his culture. He constantly refers to the Father as his model for speaking, for acting, for desiring (John 6:38, 57, 7:18, 8:28–29).

In John 8 the different models are specifically named and contrasted. Humans either imitate a model that loves or a model that kills - a model that builds up or a model that destroys. But to expose the false model he has to lure it from its unconscious den. In this conversation Jesus exposes the nature of evil as he explicitly states the connection between lies, accusation, perverted desire and collective murder.

He starts with a shocking statement to the very ones who have placed their trust in him essentially saying that they remain blindly enslaved to perverted desires and their only hope of freedom is in coming to a knowledge of truth (John 8:31-33). Freedom is not found in some privileged lineage or race. Despite being Abraham's descendants their intentions are still to kill (v40). They are equally deceived, together with every other people group, equally caught up in a murderous cycle that they can't even recognize. We seem to presume that we are free simply because we are conscious of our beliefs, choices and actions. However, as long as we remain unaware of the underlying movements that motivate and determine these beliefs and choices, we remain in bondage to our blindness.

These "disciples" protest: "*Abraham is our father.*"
Jesus responds with a sobering conclusion: Your action reveals who/what birthed your intentions and desires.
They protest even stronger: "*we have only one father, God himself.*" (v41).
Jesus replies: "*If God were your Father, you would love ...*"

The God Jesus knows as Father does not murder nor sacrifice the innocent. This God loves! The God known by Jesus is not caught up in the cycle of revenge or retributive justice. Love is our authentic and true model, whereas the accuser is the deceptive false model.

> *Why do you not understand what I say? It is because you cannot bear to hear my word. You are of your father the devil, and your will is to do your father's desires. He was a murderer from the beginning, and does not stand in the truth, because there is no truth in him. When he lies, he speaks out of his own character, for he is a liar and the father of lies.*
> (John 8:43–44 ESV)

The real source of evil is the lies we are unconsciously bound by. What drives people to violence (causing suffering), even to murder in the name of God, is a mindset birthed by accusation - the devil. (The devil is the Greek equivalent to the Hebrew satan). As such they are captivated by desires and bound to fulfill intentions of which the source is not recognized by them. These "disciples" are modeling accusation and as such the accuser, better known as the devil.

Notice that Jesus does NOT say that the devil was a beautiful and perfect angel in the beginning, but then he became proud and rebelled.
No!
Jesus does not participate in our efforts to veil evil with magical stories. He is exposing evil for what it is. *"He was a murderer from the beginning, and does not stand in the truth, because there is no truth in him."*

Our unconscious false assumptions and their conscious violent results are the very foundations upon which we have built our societies. Jesus is busy stripping the mythical figure of the devil, exposing the fact that it is deception and violence that lies at the heart of evil. These principalities and powers would soon converge to annihilate Jesus.

Every part of the mimetic cycle is being exposed: The blindness that is part of the very fabric of human societies since their inception, the models we reflect and the desires they awaken, the unresolved conflicts and frustration that need to find relief by projecting our own evils onto others.

PART OF A PATTERN

In the light of exposing evil's murderous beginning, how did Jesus understand his imminent death?

Woe to you, scribes and Pharisees, hypocrites, because you clean off the outside of the cup and the plate while inside they are full of greed and self-indulgence. You blind Pharisee! First clean the inside of the cup, so that its outside may become clean too. "Woe to you, scribes and Pharisees, hypocrites, because you are like whitewashed tombs that look beautiful on the outside but on the inside are full of dead men's bones and all kinds of filth. So you also outwardly appear to others as righteous but within you are full of hypocrisy and lawlessness. "Woe to you, scribes and Pharisees, hypocrites, because you build the tombs of the prophets and decorate the graves of the righteous, and you say, 'If we had lived in the days of our fathers, we would not have taken part with them in shedding the blood of the prophets.' By saying this you testify against yourselves that you are descendants of those who murdered the prophets. Fill up then the measure of your fathers' guilt. You snakes! You brood of vipers! How will you escape from being condemned to hell? Therefore I am sending you prophets and wise men and scribes, some of whom you will kill and crucify, and some of whom you will flog in your synagogues and pursue from town to town, so that upon you will come all the righteous blood shed

on earth, from the blood of righteous Abel to the blood of Zechariah son of Barachiah, whom you murdered between the sanctuary and the altar. I tell you the truth, all these things will come upon this generation.
(Matthew 23:25–36 Mounce)

In this passage Jesus places his own death not on some unique pedestal but in line with a long list of unjust murders. His death is part of an existing pattern and will retell this ancient story in which the innocent are victimized by the self-righteous. Their graves were decorated and whitewashed, even revered by later generations. However, inside these sacred graves lay hidden the horror of violence and unjust murder. What a clear picture of the sacrificial system. We have whitewashed these graves with our sacred stories and myths, stories that hid the reality within, with all kinds of decorative language.

We had to justify the communities we had built upon innocent blood. In the rare moments in which we recognized the unjust nature of our societies and the innocence of our victims, we distanced ourselves from those who built our civilizations saying: "*If we had lived in the days of our fathers, we would not have taken part with them in shedding the blood*". And so we remain hypocrites never recognizing the source of this evil. Evil is not in some other place and time. Evil is not limited to other people.

Evil arises within the perverted mimetic cycle which is woven into our societies.

In Luke 11:44 Jesus compares them to unmarked tombs who people walk over without recognizing. The very foundations of our societies remain unrecognized. The myth of redemptive violence remains unchallenged. Jesus comes to reveal what was kept hidden since the foundation of our world. He comes to retell our story and pause at every point at which we try to obscure the truth in order to unveil the reality of what is actually happening.

ESCALATING CONFLICT

The mimetic cycle intensifies as more people are drawn into the conflict. Accusations increase and a number of attempts are made on Jesus' life. The tension is reaching boiling point.

[M]any of the Jews who had come with Mary and seen what he had done, believed in him. Some of them, however, went to the Pharisees and told them what Jesus had done. So the chief priests and the Pharisees gathered the Council together and said, "What are we going to do? For this man is performing many signs. If we let him go on like this, everyone will believe in him, and the Romans will come and destroy both our holy place and our nation." But one of them, Caiaphas, who was high priest that year, said to them, "You know nothing at all. Or do you not

realize that it is to your advantage that one man should die for the people and that the whole nation should not perish?" He did not say this on his own, but being high priest that year he was prophesying that Jesus was about to die for the nation, and not only for the nation, but that he should gather into one the children of God who were scattered abroad. So from that day on they planned to put him to death.

(John 11:45–53 Mounce)

The council members seem to still be hesitating between differing opinions. There is no clear way of dealing with the crisis. Caiaphas brings clarity and gives direction to the confused intentions of the council. For the sake of preserving the community, Jesus has to die. Whereas myths hide the real reasons behind sacrifice, notice how the gospels expose them. The guilt or innocence of the victim is arbitrary. What is important is maintaining the status quo. The solution has been decided, it is now simply a matter of time.

Crowds begin to arrive in Jerusalem for the Passover feast. The Roman military is on alert. These occasions have seen mob violence before. The rumors of Jesus have spread as well and many are anxious to see him... but will he come in the midst of such tension?

The next day the large crowd that had come to the festival, on hearing that Jesus was coming to Jerusalem, took branches of palm trees and went out to meet him. They began to cry out, 'Hosanna! Blessed in the name of the Lord is the coming one, even the king of Israel!' ... The Pharisees therefore said to one another, 'You see, you are accomplishing nothing. Look, the world has gone after him!'

(John 12:12–19 Mounce)

If Jesus had any intention of starting a violent revolution, he had every opportunity to do so. How to fulfill his vocation as be the 'Son of Man' is something Jesus thought and prayed much about. As crowds gather and tensions increase, he already knows the path he is to take.

As long as the crowds are not united, tension continues to escalate. The gospels show us how all parties are gradually swept up in mimetic crisis. Cracks begin to appear among Jesus' own disciples. Judas makes a deal with the chief priests and begins to look for an opportunity to betray Jesus. (Mt 26:16)

Peter makes the brave announcement:

"I will lay down my life for you."

Jesus replied, "Will you lay down your life for me? I tell you the solemn truth, the rooster will not crow before you deny me three times."
(John 13:38 Mounce)

Even those closest to Jesus are not immune to the power of the crowd drawing everyone into its perverted mimetic cycle. Peter eventually swears upon hearing the name of Jesus and denies knowing him. The purpose of these stories is not to give us psychological insights into individuals, but to show that everyone without exception is swept along with the crowd - bound to obey a system of intimidation.

The contradiction of this situation: a good and innocent man, Jesus, knowingly giving himself into the hands of an unjust, lying, betraying and murderous mob, is almost unbearable. This might be why we often ignore this tension. We speak of the cross as God's plan and purpose in such a way that we remain blind to the evil forces at work to callously betray, unjustly accuse, and finally murder him.

REDEMPTIVE VIOLENCE?

Why would Jesus follow this path of suffering - why the cross? Did he perceive it as the only way to satisfy his Father's sense of justice? Or does he somehow derive pleasure from his pain? Is there some mystical redemptive value in suffering? Does Jesus believe in redemptive violence?

Throughout his whole life Jesus alleviated the suffering of others. He delighted in life, and all who came into contact with him became more alive! The lame and cripple rose up into a greater fullness of life - a greater celebration of their humanity. The blind and deaf had their senses given back to them. Jesus never showed any desire to humiliate or reduce human existence through suffering, but rather, brought us back to our senses to experience life fully as the joyful, generous gift of God. "*I came that they may have and enjoy life, and have it in abundance (to the full, till it overflows)*" (John 10:10 AMP).

His delight in life and his message of the value and dignity of being human makes the event of the cross such a contradiction to his story. It is clear from the text that Jesus, although he knew it was necessary, did not want to die and was obviously afraid of what lay ahead. He earnestly sought for another way. "*And He took with Him Peter and James and John, and began to be struck with terror and amazement and deeply troubled and depressed. And He said to them, My soul is exceedingly sad (overwhelmed with grief) so that it almost kills Me! Remain here and keep awake and be watching*" (Mark 14:33–34 AMP).

Jesus did not have a masochistic, perverted enjoyment of suffering.
So again we ask, why the cross?
Was it that the Father required it?

We have established that Jesus had no delight in violence, blood or the annihilation of human life, but maybe the Father does. As a human, Jesus personally knew the pain and anguish that awaited, but maybe the Father could remain unmoved by such temporal technicalities in order to satisfy some greater ideal. After all, when Jesus finishes his desperate prayer for another way, he ends the conversation by saying: "*Abba, Father, all things are possible for you. Remove this cup from me. Yet not what I will, but what you will.*" (Mark 14:36 ESV).

Was it simply the frailty of human existence that caused Jesus' will to seemingly differ from the Father's will at this moment of crises? That is certainly the way many have read it.

What I want to establish is the active roles of Father, Son and humanity in the actual event of the crucifixion.

Jesus knowingly and voluntarily surrenders himself into the hands of those who would murder him, into the social cycle that demands a sacrifice, the religion whose purity codes demand death.

Similarly the Father "*gave up*" the Son. "*He who did not spare his own Son but **gave him up** for us all*" (Romans 8:32 ESV). He was "*delivered up*" or "*handed over*". "*This Jesus, **delivered up** according to the definite plan and* *foreknowledge of God, you crucified and killed by the hands of lawless men."* (Acts 2:23 ESV). "*[W]ho was delivered up for our trespasses and raised for our justification.*" (Romans 4:25 ESV).

These texts make it clear that Jesus' role is in surrendering himself; the Father hands his son over into the hands of those who will torture, crucify and murder him. It is not God the Father nor the Son who plays any active role in the brutal violence that follows. Rather, it is here in the midst of sacrificial violence that our acts are most devoid of God's presence. He "*hands over*" precisely because He does not participate in the violence to follow. It is here where humanity(represented by Jesus) is handed over to itself, where God withdraws, where man does what man alone can do, for God has no part in our violence.

But if Jesus takes no pleasure in such a suffering death and the Father does not participate in the violence, and neither does the Spirit who is the comforter… then why does Jesus voluntarily choose this way?

The miracles cease and the teachings stop for both are impotent against the greatest enemy - the fear of death. It is in the midst of a mob who tries to mask their fear of death, by killing, that Jesus refuses to bow to fear. The fear that infects the crowd is the most original fear: the underlying anxiety that we deserve death as a form of punishment.

However, when Jesus previously spoke of his imminent death, he did not speak of it as the necessary punishment required by some higher form of justice but rather as the highest form of love (John 15:13). But how then is this death an act of love? It is here where Jesus faces our greatest fear for us and overcomes it. What is redemptive in this drama of the cross is not the suffering or the violence but it is the trust with which Jesus overcomes fear. It is his trust in the Father, energized by his love for his friends, that strengthens him to face our deepest fears on our behalf and conquer them!

Jesus surrenders himself into our rage and the Father hands over the Son into our blind cycle of violence, for it is only from within that our confusion can be subverted and our violence can be exposed as belonging to ourselves alone. He willingly becomes the sacrificial victim to save us from sacrifice and the violent god-images birthed by it. He undoes our myths from within. He enters into the very heart of our anxieties - the fear that we are not accepted, that we are not worthy of life - and there he shows us a God who unconditionally accepts and embraces our humanity. And so it is while we are at our worst, while we are enemies, that he reconciles us (Romans 5:10).

If it is simply suffering and death that is redemptive, then sickness or any other means of death would have been sufficient. But there is a deeper logic at work. God makes use of this specific occasion, this kind of death inflicted by a community in chaos, to address our most fundamental sin: our misinterpretation of the intentions of God, and the murderous results it has in the scapegoating mechanism. Scapegoating is the way in which we transform our own sense of inadequacy into the guilt of another and joining with a community who does the same, we rid ourselves of the guilty party. In so doing we temporarily alleviate our inner chaos. It is therefore precisely this kind of death that symbolizes our misunderstanding of God most accurately.

THE DRAMA CONTINUES

So Jesus is following a path which He knows will lead to a painful death. He is knowingly stepping into the position of the sacrificial victim. Jesus does this not because he finds pleasure in pain or because his Father requires it, but because we require it. Our alienation can only be undone from within. When the opportunity finally comes for Judas, together with a large crowd, to betray him with a kiss, his disciples still seem to be ready for a fight. One of them grabs a sword and swings at the servant of the high priest. The servant probably ducked just in time because only his ear is cut off! Jesus diffuses the situation by telling him to put his sword away ... "*for all who take the sword will perish by the sword ... but all this happened that the scripture and the prophets might be fulfilled*" (Matthew 26:52,56).

Overcoming violence with violence has never resulted in a kingdom of peace. At this point Jesus seems to be keenly mindful of specific scriptures that need to be fulfilled. (v54, 56) We don't know with certainty what scriptures he was thinking of, but we do know that the day before he was thinking of Zechariah 9 when he specifically found a young donkey on which to enter Jerusalem. The prophesy continues to speak of this king of peace entering Jerusalem and doing away with all weapons of war as he introduces us to the peace of God.

Jesus hands himself over and the disciples flee, for it seems to be the only alternative. He is escorted to the courtyard of the high priest. "*Now the chief priest and the whole council were seeking false testimony against Jesus that they might put him to death, but they found none*" (Matthew 26:59). Again, the gospels make the innocence of our sacrificial victims clear.

The next morning Jesus is brought before Pilate and we once again see the power of the mimetic cycle to absorb everyone, no matter what their status, into its influence.

Pilate himself is also ruled by mimetic contagion. He would prefer to spare Jesus. If the Gospels insist upon this preference, it is not to suggest that the Romans are superior to the Jews, in other words: to allot good and bad points to the persecutors of Jesus. It is rather to underscore the paradox of the sovereign power that surrenders to the crowd and melts into it, as it were, for fear of an encounter with it. The account this shows once again the omnipotence of mimetic contagion. What motivates Pilate, as he hands over Jesus, is the fear of a riot.[3]

THE SINGLE VICTIM MECHANISM

Crowds gather and chaos increases as a multitude of conflicts and tensions reach their culmination. This could end in disaster - indiscriminate violence can erupt at any moment. Suddenly all of the frustrations begin to solidify and become focused on the one person who showed so much promise, yet so deeply disappointed their expectations. The war of all against all, as conflict rages between all the opposing parties, becomes a war of all against one.

MAN'S JUDGMENT OF JESUS

Pilate knew that Jesus was innocent (John 18:38; 19:4,6), but he was captive to obey another system. The reason he hands Jesus over is explicit: he feared the crowds (John 19:12,13). Ciaiphas' judgment reveals the same motivation for condemning Jesus - He feared that Jesus would persuade the crowd. The power of the crowd, the contagious mimetic cycle, is what stirs terror in these figures of power. Their understanding of power leaves them with only two choices:

---

3   Rene Girard, I See Satan Fall Like Lightning, Page 20

stir up and unite the crowd against a scapegoat, or become the chosen scapegoat by opposing the crowd.

It is not an uncivilized mob or an irreligious crowd that condemns Jesus to death. It is the very representatives of civilization and religion that murder him. And so, human judgment exposes the emptiness of our wisdom as it reveals the fragmented, unstable and murderous foundations upon which we build societies.

It is not the judgment of God, but mankind's judgment that condemns Jesus to death. The murder of the innocent man Jesus Christ can never be justified – it was wrong! He was falsely accused and brutally abused by a frenzied, ignorant crowd. Nowhere else was the true nature of our religious and secular institutions more clearly revealed than in this senseless violence. This is where God in all his innocence, and in his most vulnerable state, faces evil in its most articulate expression – the unjustified violence of man. Evil incarnate meets God incarnate. The God who is love meets the deception that murders... and forgives, *for they know not what they do.*

GOD'S JUDGMENT OF THIS WORLD

Now is the judgment of this world; now will the ruler of this world be cast out.
(John 12:31 ESV)

But we impart a secret and hidden wisdom of God, which
God decreed before the ages for our glory. None of the
rulers of this age understood this, for if they had, they
would not have crucified the Lord of glory.
(1 Corinthians 2:7–8 ESV)

It is the act of crucifixion, the very judgment mankind pronounced on Jesus, that is transformed into God's judgment of the ruler of this world as the principalities and powers are unwittingly exposing themselves for what they truly are. Mankind's judgment is inversed and becomes our undoing.

Here the justice of man would be exposed as injustice as it met the forgiveness that restores. This is where the strength of Empires would meet the weakness of God. In this meeting the weakness of the Empire's strength would be exposed, and the power of God's weakness would be revealed, for *"the weakness of God is stronger than men"* (1 Cor 1:25).

Yet it is exactly here where evil is most real that God intersects, turning our act of murder into our salvation. He uses the occasion of our most brutal violence to demonstrate His most extravagant love. He bore the brunt of our hostile minds, of our sinful thoughts. The event in which we bruised him and wounded him is met with healing. At the very moment in which our rejection of him is absolute he demonstrates our absolute and unconditional forgiveness and acceptance.

GOD'S JUDGMENT OF JESUS

Mankind's judgment of Jesus results in his death. God's judgment of Jesus results in his resurrection. God vindicates the message and person of Jesus by raising him from the dead and exalting him to a place of unparalleled honor.

We have often ascribed both the good and the evil of the cross to God! Let's expose that myth:

God obviously anticipated these events. He knew that the open display of truth in a world bound by myth would be a confrontation with only one possible result. The very fabric upon which our societies were built, the false accusation, the prince (principle) of this world, the father of lies, would not take to this exposure kindly. Yes, God knew and planned to make the most of this confrontation, but in no way is He the source of the violence that it exposes. In no way does He delight in the suffering and death of Jesus Christ.

Whenever the apostles speak about the death and resurrection of Christ they assign responsibility for the two events to two different parties. Peter says:

But you denied the Holy One and the Just, and asked for a murderer to be granted to you, and killed the Prince of life, whom God raised from the dead, of which we are witnesses. (Acts 3:14,15)

Him, being delivered by the determined purpose and foreknowledge of God, you have taken by lawless hands, have crucified, and put to death; whom God raised up (Acts 2:23,24)

We can go on and on - the scriptural witness is consistent: You(man) killed him - God raised Him.

"*you crucified him*" (Acts 2:36)
"*you rejected him*" (3:14)
"*you crucified*" (4:10)
"*you have now betrayed and murdered*" (7:52)
"*Jesus, whom you had killed...*" (5:30)

BUT God raised Him up!

Man does the killing and God does the making-alive!
Our judgment of Jesus resulted in his condemnation to death. God's judgment resulted in his justification and resurrection.

THE FOUNDING MURDER AND MYTH UNDONE
Jesus' last teaching would be done without words. He takes us back to the event that gave birth to our myths - our perverted ideas about who God is and how to solve our

societal conflicts. He enters our conversation as deeply as he possibly can by taking the part of the sacrificial victim. He does not give us a theory of atonement; he demonstrates his at-one-ment with us even in our deepest confusion and alienation from him.

It is in the actual event that our deceptive language is undone as we come face to face with the reality of what actually happened:

Our stories tell of a guilty individual (or minority group) who is justly sacrificed by a righteously indignant community. The cross reveals the innocence of our conveniently chosen scapegoats and the guilt of the murdering mob.

Our sacred stories tell of gods who delight in the just punishment of the guilty, realized in the actual spilling of their blood in the ritual of sacrifice. The cross reveals a God, who would rather suffer our violence than partake in it. He would rather become the victim of our injustice than enforce our type of retributive justice upon us.

Our myths demonize our victims, conveniently locating evil in selected individuals. The consequence is a belief that if we can get rid of evil people, we can get rid of evil. The cross exposes evil as a cycle of perverted reflections in which both victims and victimizers are caught.

Even our later Christian stories (some variations of atonement theory) view the cross as the place in which God the Father satisfies His righteous indignation by punishing His son with the just wages of sin - death. However, if God the Father was nailing anything to that cross, it was not His son but the very law of retribution. The very system that demands retributive justice is exposed and nullified by God. It was the very document that demanded our punishment that was nailed to that cross according to Colossians 2:14! And it is while we are nailing him to that cross that he prays for our forgiveness (Luke 22:34).

Jesus retells the human drama from the viewpoint of its victims because perpetrators of evil see themselves most clearly through the eyes of their victims. But if victims only see themselves through the eyes of their oppressors, they will in turn become oppressors. Both the victims and those who injured them need a greater reference than one another to be free.

When anthropologists began to catalogue the various myths of dying and rising gods to be found across cultures, and lumped the Jesus story in with them, some Christians reacted in outrage. They insisted that this disparaged Jesus' importance and contended that he did not belong in that company. One notable exception was the apologist C. S. Lewis. Lewis knew the world's mythological heritage far better than most. He maintained that the match was a good one, that in fact the myths and the Gospels were telling the same story. The only difference was that this story became fact only once, in Jesus. As he put it, "The old myth of the Dying God, without ceasing to be myth, comes down from the heaven of legend and imagination to the earth of history. It happens - at a particular date, in a particular place, followed by definable historical consequences. We pass from a Baldur or an Osiris, dying nobody knows when or where, to an historical Person crucified ... under Pontius Pilate." There was more to Lewis's point than he realized. He saw that the redeemer myths were about an unreal demigod "dying" in some indeterminate time and place. It was only a story, while Jesus was flesh and blood. But we are suggesting that behind the mythical stories there were actually also flesh and blood victims. Jesus' cross wasn't the one time it happened. It was the time we knew it happened, and became able to see others.[4]

Jesus became one with real victims as he became the ultimate innocent victim of injustice. In our identification with Him on that cross, we see evil for what it is – we see ourselves through the eyes of our innocent victim. But in His resurrection He deprives the murderer (humanity) of their victim. In our identification with Him in His resurrection, we see love for what it is – we see ourselves

---

4   Mark S. Heim. Saved from Sacrifice: A Theology of the Cross (Locations 1506-1514). Kindle Edition.

not as victims demanding revenge but as victors over evil, offering forgiveness. Unlike the blood of many innocent victims His blood does not cry for vengeance but for forgiveness.

We have all been victims and we have all been victimizers. Victims can become obsessed with their victimizers, and perpetrators of violence can become obsessed with their victims as both are caught in hate and shame. If we only see each other we will forever be caught up in this circle of violence.

The message of Jesus breaks this circle of evil by giving us a new reference for who we are. The victim is no longer a victim if he or she chooses forgiveness instead of revenge. The victimizer no longer needs to live in the shame of his or her evil as they receive forgiveness. Jesus introduces us to our true mirror – the God in whose image and likeness we were created to reflect dignity, love and the courage to be our true selves even in the midst of a perverse world.

13 - Zombie Apocalypse!

The crowds disperse. The tensions cease. But for those who knew Jesus, the silent days that follow the crucifixion are filled with grief. The empire has once again proven the effectiveness of its methods. It has won the argument in the most convincing way - by silencing the opposition forever.

The pain of witnessing their friend's brutal death does not go away, but slowly makes room for deep disillusion. So much of who they thought they were, was interwoven with who they thought Jesus was. Much of their relationships with each other were centered in this relationship with the one they thought was the Messiah, but he turned out to be nothing of what they expected. He is gone... and so are the illusionary identities and relationships that were based on his person. The surreal events of the past couple of days begin to dissipate in the light of the very harsh reality of this world. Jesus' inspirational messages of love begin to fade from memory as they have been proven to be nothing but idealistic sentimentalities.

If not for the resurrection event, the life, teachings and death of Jesus would most likely have disappeared into obscurity. His death would have been just one more act of violence, one more scapegoat forever silenced by the ruling mob. None of his followers would have been eager to record his life events and sayings, for in doing so they would relive the embarrassing teachings of the one who so deeply disappointed them.

Following his death there was a period of shocked silence among Jesus' followers. But the resurrected Jesus Christ shocks his disciples out of a silence of disappointment into a silence of amazement as this event exceeds all expectations, all language and all forms of expression. This is, however, a silence from which they recover. Although it is with stammering lips at first, they soon discover that what they witnessed is irrepressible; it must be declared.

UNEXPECTED

Peter is the first to boldly declare the resurrection of Jesus Christ. However, the declaration that the one we murdered has been made alive by God cannot be good news! Those who first heard it were "cut to the heart" and asked "what shall we do?"

Only a couple of weeks before, Jesus told the story of evil stewards who murdered all the messengers sent by the landlord and finally they murdered the son also. According to their own judgment such evil men had to be utterly destroyed! (Mt. 21:41) The memory of their own judgment suddenly takes on grave new meaning. The realization dawns that they are the wicked servants who murdered the son!

What can we expect from a resurrected victim? Revenge! There will be hell to pay! This can only be the ultimate zombie apocalypse!

The one we judged guilty and worthy of death was judged by God to be innocent and consequently God raised him from the dead. And to make matters worse, God has exalted him to be the judge! (Acts 10:42, 43) This means that we were not innocently co-operating with God to restore order to our society by crucifying this troublemaker, but rather, we opposed God by murdering His son!

We can therefore expect nothing less than retribution from both our victim and our victim's Father, who turns out to be none less than God himself!

Against all expectation Peter presents to them their victim coming towards them, not with vengeance, but with a smile, with arms open wide and forgiveness on his lips.

The logical response to violent injustice is vengeance or, as some would call it, retributive justice. What normally followed the execution of a leader who had messianic ambitions was disillusioned followers who either scattered or, in some cases, reformed to take revenge. But the resurrection of Jesus undoes the naturally expected effect.

RESURRECTION AS EVENT

The resurrection is an event like no other.

Everything takes on new meaning in the light of this event. Most events happen in such a way that we are able to discern their cause and effect. We can analyze the event objectively, date it and associate certain facts with it. We may even personally experience the event and add it to our list of "been there, done that". It becomes an experience we've had, a memory we may cherish… or try to forget. But there are events of a different class and magnitude. We don't simply experience these events and then continue on with our lives. These events remain present in a way. The experience is too large to simply "have had it"; its more than historic; it changes everything it touches. Falling in love or the death of a loved one might be placed in this category.

The resurrection however is an event beyond any of these categorizations. It happens outside of the logic of cause and effect. A brutal murder does not logically lead to a resurrected physical body. The effect of this event is beyond the grasp of any calculation. Yes, we can attempt to analyze it… and we should. We can date it fairly accurately. Many facts related to the event can add further insight. We may even begin to experience the overwhelming reality of it beyond these historic facts - an experience that we never fully possess but rather an experience we allow to possess us. Yet it always remains more than what we have articulated or experienced so far.

The resurrection is an event of such enormous significance that it saturates all of time with new meaning. The past becomes illuminated with an understanding that was simply not present before this event. The sayings of Jesus begin to make sense for the first time. Even his meaningless and disturbing death becomes drenched in value and comfort. This is not another event limited to a specific date and restricted to objective meaning. Its meaning continues to unfold.

> *This ongoing, inexhaustible event of his death, and resurrection is not contained within the linear print of any book— nor in the sum total of all the books of the world (John 21: 25). Hence, genuine faith is not engaged in a video replay of the highlights of the game once one's team has won. It is not a matter of reproducing impressions or trying to capture a dwindling after-effect, but of entering, however disoriented and tongue-tied, into an involvement with what causes everything to be made and seen anew.[1]*

The future becomes filled with the same surprising possibilities as this event in which all limits have been removed. All of time becomes new as past, present and

1   Violence, Desire, and the Sacred (p. 72). Bloomsbury Academic. Kindle Edition.

future are redefined. This is the beginning of a new creation; the beginning of a whole new human story that undoes the mythical stories.

JESUS AND MYTHS OF DYING AND RISING GODS

Myths of dying and rising divinities have been present in primitive societies all over the world.

> *In the great cult celebrations there stand ... at the centre, in connection with all manner of different occasions, the repetition of mythical events of the origins; it emerges clearly from this that human and animal sacrifices, maturity and fertility cults and other ceremonies and ritual customs are not individual cultural elements, which have come together more or less accidentally in a cultural group, but that they are all derived from a central idea, namely, that of a divinity who was killed and who by his death established the present order of existence of the world.[2]*

A quick reminder of how these myths originated: The problem of chaos and violence in early communities was not solved by rational arguments. Rather, in the midst of irrational rage, the solution spontaneously presented itself as the conflict of all against all turned into a conflict of all against one. Through the single victim mechanism a magical peace arrived. The actors in this mimetic cycle were

2   Jensen 1966 - quoted from Jesus in the Drama of Salvation, by Raymond Schwager, page 127

so blinded by passion that the whole process that produced the peace remained a mystery to them. Peace followed the chaos as indiscriminate violence was replaced by a new kind of sacred violence. The victim was credited for both the chaos and the peace and so was perceived as the source of both curse and blessing. This experience of both blessing and curse simultaneously present is what Ethnologists[3] describe as the universal experience of the sacred. Behind the myths are real events, real victims.

How does Jesus' story compare to these myths?

Jesus, in solidarity with all victims, was driven out of the community by a murderous mob and killed. The process and tensions that lead up to this crisis are the same. In the myths, there is an immediate transition from chaos to peace at the moment of sacrifice. Consequently the demonized victim is transformed into a heroic divinity. The stories that explain this transition are told by the survivors.

In contrast, through the resurrection of Jesus it is the victim who tells the story and consequently unveils the self-deception present in the myths. Blind rage is revealed as exactly that - a condition of ignorance. "*Father forgive them for they know not what they are doing.*" The gospel draws a clear distinction between the action of mankind

---

3   Ethnology is the branch of anthropology that compares and analyzes the characteristics of different peoples and the relationship between them (cf. cultural, social, or sociocultural anthropology).

who murdered Jesus and the action of God who raised him from the dead.

The myths also tell of the altars that were built over the sacrificial corpse. The most primitive of such sacred sites might simply have been the pile of stones that lay over the stoned victim. On a more sophisticated level, it might well be this image of piled stones that was later revered in the building of the pyramids. The sacred grave is the first visible sign of a new culture. These sealed tombs also bear witness to a veiled understanding - a phenomenon that worked, but we could not see why.

In contrast, the resurrected Jesus leaves behind an empty tomb, an open grave. Through it he unveils the processes that gave us our sense of the sacred. The open grave is a new foundation for a new community, a new culture, a new humanity - one that is not built upon ignorant violence but inspired forgiveness.

JESUS ENTERED OUR MYTHS

The many narratives we have developed throughout our history have simply retold a basic story. The death of Jesus brings all these stories to a dead-end. Our theories, theologies and philosophies weren't getting progressively better; they just re-hashed our delusions from different angles. Every avenue we took and every direction our conversations explored were still caught in this inescapable cycle in which we simply reflected our own fears and hopes. No wonder Paul reminds us that God came to nullify our wisdom (1 Corinthians 1:25).

The cross brings our stories to an end. It exposes the meaningless conclusions to all our myths. Similarly, the cross is not the glorious culmination of human history or of Jewish history - Jesus fulfills our history by bringing it to an end. God was not controlling and directing human history towards this climactic event. Rather, God breaks into our broken history, into the chaos of these scattered events, to bring it to a final end.

It is only when our own ideas have finally ceased, when our history has exhausted itself in its pursuit of meaning, when evil has done its worst, when we have reached the ultimate end - the death of God, that a truly new creation, a truly new time, a truly new story can begin. He entered our conversations so deeply that he became one with our myths and suffered their tragic end in his death. It is precisely here, where all our stories cease, that a truly new story can begin.

In this context, the resurrection is the truly new event that breaks the cycle of repetitive time where chaos and order, profane violence and sacred violence, victims and victimizers continually follow in one another's footsteps on the never-ending journey of retributive justice. The resurrection is God's initiative to break into our world and so help us break free from our myths. Jesus is transformed from demonized victim to divine hero not through blind speculation by a murderous mob who has to justify itself but by God's initiative. The bodily resurrection stands in stark contrast to the metaphorical resurrections found in myth. Let's look a bit deeper at the significance of the resurrected body of Jesus.

THE SIGNIFICANCE OF A BODILY RESURRECTION

The body is a symbol of a presence. A symbol is more than a sign. A sign points to somewhere or something else. The sign is evidence that the actual entity is not present and so the sign points beyond itself to where the entity is present. A symbol, however, can be more than a sign in that it represents the presence of the entity and participates in the reality of what it symbolizes.

For example, a sign pointing towards Seattle is only useful as long as we have not reached our destination. Once we are in Seattle, we no longer need the sign. A symbol such as a country's flag, however, represents the country. Similarly, an ambassador represents a country. He or she is the symbol of the presence of the country not of its absence. The only way in which the country can be present is through the ambassador.

Your body is the symbol of your presence. As such it does not point to an entity that is somewhere else, but rather, this symbol is the only way in which you can be present. It is the zone in which relationship becomes most real and most tangible. It is where communication is most immediate, the field in which encounters between self and others are felt most intimately.

This is what makes a corpse or a dead body so disturbing. The very symbol of a presence becomes the symbol of an absence in this lifeless stage. While the person was alive, many connections and relationships converged in this living body. In death, these relational bonds need to be reconfigured in the absence of the person, symbolized by the dead body. This might be why it is often more difficult for people who have lost a loved one and have not seen the corpse to find closure. Seeing the dead body, the symbol of their absence, can be an essential part of dealing with such a loss.

In this light it is significant that Mary sought the body (corpse) of Jesus but could not find it. A physical, dead body would be evidence of his absence. But what Mary finds is the one who could say her name like no other - one who is present. There is no corpse, no dead body, because He is not absent! He is present... and speaking *your* name! In the presence of a corpse, which symbolizes the absence of the person, all relationships need to be re-ordered. The bodily resurrection means that the relationships he had with his followers need not be reconfigured on the basis of his absence, but rather that relationship continues to be centered in the living person of the present resurrected Jesus.

The body is what gives each of us distinction and personal consistency. The bodily resurrection of Jesus Christ therefore means that our faith and relationship are not based on a Christ principle, but rather, with the same person that lived and walked with the first disciples.

THE NEW COMMUNITY

Upon this image of an open grave and a present victim, a new community is born - a community no longer bound by a mimetic cycle they do not grasp but a community who now clearly sees through the eyes of their victim. Whereas previous communities are enclosed in their own little self-referential worlds, bound to defend the borders of their small existence and justifying whatever victims they produced, the new community, which is founded on an open tomb, continually opens up and expands to include outcasts. As long as this community is centered on the ever unfolding event of the death and resurrection of Christ Jesus, it continues to be surprised by the boundless goodness of God.

NATURE OF THE RESURRECTED BODY

During the period between the resurrection and ascension, Jesus manifested himself in bodily form on a number of occasions to individuals and groups. What was the nature of these appearances and why are they significant?

These manifestations happened unexpectedly and in some cases to unlikely candidates. These are not dreams or visions but happen in the middle of the day, in the midst of ordinary life and in most cases to more than one person. The sheer number and diversity of manifestations make it unlikely that it was some sort of hallucination that spread contagiously. On a few occasions, people didn't recognize him until he explicitly identified himself to them as with Mary at the tomb and the disciples on the road to Emmaus.

From these witnesses we can conclude that Jesus chooses when and how to materialize himself. It happens by his own initiative and is not a self-induced vision on the part of the seer. These events are objectively experienced. Yet, these happenings were more than natural objective events. Jesus not only materialized but he also had to open the eyes of those present to recognize him. The participants knew that they witnessed more than a physical reality, more than a natural phenomenon within the boundaries of space and time.

In short, there is a bodily reality that is not an ordinary, natural, physical body. But it is also not an invisible spirit or a group consciousness of some kind. The glorified Jesus, as he appears to his disciples, is a singular, personal, and perceptible agent who is numerically identical with the One who died on the cross on Good Friday and who interacts with his disciples who are still in this world and subject to the conditions of historical existence. We are dealing with historical experience (that of the disciples) of non-historical reality (the glorified Jesus) somehow mediated by body (which is what we mean by the risen Jesus).[4]

Remember, the body is a symbol of a presence. The resurrected Jesus can symbolize himself, materialize his body, wherever and whenever and for whatsoever purpose He chooses. He is no longer subject to time, space or physical laws, but is able to interact in our time and space at will. At every one of the extraordinary appearances between the resurrection and Easter, he also prepares those who see him that his future appearances would be different - that he would be present... but in a very different kind of body.

4   Schneiders, Sandra (2014-02-27). Jesus Risen in Our Midst (Kindle Locations 534-538). The Liturgical Press. Kindle Edition.

New Spirit, New Mimesis, New Community

In John 20 we find the anxious disciples hiding themselves behind locked doors. Suddenly Jesus stands among them. It does not say that he walked through walls or locked doors … he simply materialized. He shows the shocked disciples the wounds on his hands and feet. By it he demonstrates that he is not a disembodied spirit but the same person whose crucifixion they witnessed.

> *Jesus said to them again, "Peace be with you. As the Father has sent me, even so I am sending you." And when he had said this, he breathed on them and said to them, "Receive the Holy Spirit."*
> (John 20:21–22 ESV)

In contrast to their self-enclosed world of fear, the old world of twisted desire, *for all that is in the world—the desires of the flesh and the desires of the eyes and pride of life—is not from the Father but is from the world[5]*, Jesus is opening up to them a whole new world. It is the world of the Father in which his breath is the new mimesis of self-giving love, rather than fearful rivalry. The self-referential existence of the old world has no future for that *world is passing away along with its desires, but whoever does the will of God abides forever[6]*. A new mode of existence has arrived, a new future is received as we breathe in his spirit, the same spirit that

---

5   1 John 2:16 ESV
6   1 John 2:17 ESV

enabled him to resist conformity to the world of twisted desires and instead give his life freely to his friends.

Jesus materializes himself and begins a new community, one that would be founded on his person and presence, a community not self-enclosed but ever unfolding, not energized by unconscious desires, but rather, a community that consciously models the one who visibly demonstrated what love is.

> *If you forgive the sins of any, they are forgiven them; if you retain the sins of any, they are retained.*
> (John 20:23 NKJV)

Sandra Schneiders, in her book "Jesus Risen in Our Midst" has done a thorough and beautiful analysis of this verse and concludes:

> *...the text of John 20:23 does not say anything about "retaining sins." Translated literally, it says, "Of whomever you forgive the sins, they are forgiven to them; whomever you hold are held fast."*[7]

In other words, just as the Father sent Jesus (to take away the sin of the world), even so Jesus is sending us to forgive and dissolve the last residues of sin as we embrace the world the way he embraced us. Jesus took away the sin,

---

7   Schneiders, Sandra (2014-02-27). Jesus Risen in Our Midst (Kindle Locations 2080-2081). The Liturgical Press. Kindle Edition.

singular, of the world, exposing the underlying deception that warped our desires, our view of God, ourselves and the world. We are now called to forgive the sins, *plural,* of the world, these are the many after effects, the thoughts and behaviors that resulted from the singular sin - our basic blindness. We continue in this new spirit, this new mimetic cycle of love, to embrace and include others in the fellowship of the Father, Son and Spirit. Regarding this new mimesis, Paul wrote: "*Watch what God does, and then you do it, like children who learn proper behavior from their parents. Mostly what God does is love you. Keep company with him and learn a life of love. Observe how Christ loved us. His love was not cautious but extravagant. He didn't love in order to get something from us but to give everything of himself to us. Love like that.*"[8]

This new mimetic cycle is contagious too. The desire of God awakens our desire, we in turn can no longer look at any person from a human point of view but recognize in them the same beauty God recognizes in us. Our fear-locked rooms are transformed into ever expanding faith-filled adventures. He fills these rooms with a presence that cannot remain stagnant in that old cycle of retribution, but finds ever new expression in embracing and forgiving a world desperately in need of such love.

---

8   Ephesians 5:1–2 MESSAGE

The very nature of Christ's resurrected body is being transformed by the introduction of the spirit and the formation of this new community. The way in which Jesus would choose to materialize himself in the future is through a community, appropriately called, his body. The faith that is born here is unique in that it claims the personal presence and bodily indwelling of the resurrected Jesus.

On another occasion Jesus joins two traveling disciples on the road to Emmaus. Their understanding of scripture and the harsh realities of recent events left them confused. During this conversation their confusion turns to curiosity as Jesus begins to re-interpret scripture for them.

> *So they drew near to the village to which they were going. He acted as if he were going farther, but they urged him strongly, saying, "Stay with us, for it is toward evening and the day is now far spent." So he went in to stay with them. When he was at table with them, he took the bread and blessed and broke it and gave it to them. And their eyes were opened, and they recognized him. And he vanished from their sight.*
>
> (Luke 24:28–31 ESV)

It is significant that their knowledge of scripture did not lead them to an encounter with Jesus but rather, it was an encounter with the resurrected and living Jesus Christ that helped them understand the scriptures. In the moment

248

of true recognition, Jesus disappears. Jesus disappears
not because He leaves us, but because his presence is so
close that the few feet across the table implies too much
distance! He is so present that we should no longer search
for him in another body but find him in our own... and
in the body of believers. The way in which Jesus chooses
to materialize himself is in his visible image and likeness:
mankind. Mankind is God's favorite form of existence. As
we receive and operate in this same spirit of self-giving love,
a new way of being human is unfolding. We can be human
the way Jesus was human - in harmonious union with God.

John also continually drove this message home throughout
his gospel:

*In my Father's house are many rooms (monē). If it were
not so, would I have told you that I go to prepare a place
for you? And if I go and prepare a place for you, I will
come again and will take you to myself, that where I am
you may be also.*
(John 14:2–3 ESV)

*In that day you will know that I am in my Father, and you
in me, and I in you. Whoever has my commandments and
keeps them, he it is who loves me. And he who loves me will
be loved by my Father, and I will love him and manifest
myself to him." Judas (not Iscariot) said to him, "Lord,
how is it that you will manifest yourself to us, and not to*

the world?" Jesus answered him, "If anyone loves me, he will keep my word, and my Father will love him, and we will come to him and make our home(monē) with him.
(John 14:20–23 ESV)

In this famous passage Jesus promises to go and prepare a place, a mansion (the Greek word monē), a space where both he and ourselves will be at home. What many have missed is that a few verses later he tells us exactly where that place is: "*In that day you will know that I am in my Father, and you in me, and I in you*" and then he uses the exact word for mansion used in verse 2: "*we (Jesus and His Father) will come to him and make our home(monē) with him.*"

While many dreamed of an other-worldly mansion, Jesus and the Father were dreaming of finding a home, an appropriate space for their own existence and expression, in humanity.

14 - Satan Unmasked

The crucified, yet living and present, Christ Jesus redefined and continues to redefine God, evil, me and us. In this chapter we will focus on how the cross exposed the structure of evil and how the open tomb unmasked 'Satan', for what 'it' is.

Satan - The Story So Far

There is an old Christian proverb that says: the cunning of Satan is to convince people that he does not exist. However, belief in Satan and the conviction that he must be fought has resulted in more satanic torture and murder than any other belief. Hundreds of thousands of people have been murdered, burned at the stake, drowned or tortured to death because of Christian superstitions about the devil and hell. Blind faith in the satanic is what contributed to much of the barbaric atrocities of the dark ages and continues to fuel acts of exclusion today. It seems that Satan is even more cunning than our proverb could communicate, even cunning enough to give us our proverb! Our fight against Satan is often the very way by which evil is energized. It is therefore important to know what the enemy is, so that we don't unwittingly strengthen evil through our ignorant endeavors.

In Chapter 10, *The History of Satan*, we saw that 'Satan' is an idea that developed and we can trace its history. A very real situation of enmity with an earthly foe developed into a perception of a more supernatural phenomenon. Consequently, the concept developed into an angelic being under the command of God, who is tasked to examine, accuse and act as the prosecuting attorney. The idea further matured after Israel's exile into Babylon where they were exposed to Zoroastrianism with all its accompanying ideas about an eternal struggle between forces of good and forces of evil.

Throughout the book we have looked at different ideas about God, about evil, about sacrifice and have shown how the scriptures often have multiple developing theories and theologies that do not always correspond.

Is the story of fallen angels the only story in the scriptures to explain the nature of evil?

No!

There is another!

Let me make it as plain as I can.

In what follows I will show that there is a train of thought which runs throughout the Scriptures that perceives the devil to be, not a personified character, but a principle of deceit; that understands principalities and powers to be thought structures that can manifest in actual structures of power, such as the government of Rome, rather than mythical winged spirits ruling over towns, cities and countries; that understands the satan as the kind of accusation that disrupts relationship, personally and within communities, rather than the horned, fork carrying legend of some contemporary branches of Christianity.

EXORCISING THE DEMON OF SUPERSTITION

The Genesis creation stories were written in the context of a world steeped in superstitions. Within the ancient Middle Eastern context, the gods were in constant conflict. Evil was everywhere present - in water, in earth and special combinations of these substances. The seventh day was perceived as particularly evil and so selling incantations to protect people against these evils was a profitable business. In this context of religious superstitions, the Genesis writer paints a vision of God and creation that leaves no room for magical evils. This God is the only Creator and all He made is declared to be good! On the seventh day, (the day in which superstitious people had to be particularly cautious and purchase extra protective incantations), all you need to do is chill and appreciate the goodness of what God made!

Even the snake, which was commonly associated with different destructive or fertility gods, is portrayed in the Genesis account as a creature made by God. The

Genesis creation stories were some of the most radically demythologizing writings of their time. They replaced multiplied superstitions with the one God who is distinct from, and simultaneously the source of, all creation. But if all of creation is sustained by God and declared to be good, and if there aren't supernatural evil forces lurking in natural elements, then were does evil come from?

TWISTED MIMETIC DESIRE

In chapter 3 we looked at Genesis in the context of desire. I now want to bring those thoughts to their conclusion. Evil has a human origin. If mankind did not partake of a certain kind of knowledge, one where evil and good were mixed into confusion, that turned adoration into accusation as we misinterpreted the intentions of others... then evil would have had no place in this world.

Whereas the story of the Eden temptation gives us the psychological background to sin, the story of Cain and Abel is the first recorded act of sin, namely: murder. The idea that evil arises within the human condition can be found in many scriptures.

> ... each one is tempted when he is drawn away by his own desires and enticed. Then, when desire has conceived, it gives birth to sin; and sin, when it is full-grown, brings forth death.
>
> (James 1:13-15)

Paul also locates the source of this death producing problem as "*evil desire within me*" (Romans 7:8).

UNMASKED

Our mimetic capability, perverted, became the source of individual conflict, chaos within communities, the single victim mechanism, which in turn became the basis of ritual and religion - the very basis upon which larger societies could be built.

This certainly adds much insight to Jesus' teaching on the origin of Satan.

> *He was a murderer from the beginning, and does not stand in the truth, because there is no truth in him. When he speaks a lie, he speaks from his own resources, for he is a liar and the father of it.* (John 8:44)

The cross is presented in scripture as God's victory over evil, the event in which the "*prince of this world be cast out*" (John 12:31). It is through Jesus' death that he destroyed "*him that had the power of death, that is, the devil*" (Hebrews 2:14).

If, therefore, the cross is the quintessence of God's victory over evil, sin and Satan, why is it that the passion narratives never directly mention this victory over Satan? Could it be that the very form of the satan is transformed as it is unmasked in the process of its defeat?

If the very nature of the satan is deception and the consequent ignorant violence that flows from it, then the victory of the cross lies in its ability to expose this deception. We have already seen that the function of the satanic is accusation.[1] Jesus is condemned to death by accusation. Within the passion narratives, this accusation against Jesus is based on the law. It is the very law that demands his death: "*We have a law, and by our law he ought to die, because he made himself the Son of God*" (John 19:7 KJV).

And so we see that it is not the lawless and irreligious that condemn Jesus to death, but it is through this very act that religion and the law will expose themselves for what they are.

> *Consequently the satanic appears in the gospels as a collective religious projection by means of which sinners load onto the sinless one what they do not want to see in their own hearts and so make him to be sin (2 Cor 5:21), to be cursed (Gal 3:13), to be Satan (John 19:7, 10:33) - and in this way make him the scapegoat in a new complete way.*[2]

The principle of scapegoating became the principality of this world. The power of projecting our evil gave us opportunity to deal with it in a unique but deceptive

---

1   Job 1:6-2:10, Zec 3:1

2   Raymund Schwager, Banished From Eden, page 148

way, and in many cases this lead to the extermination or expulsion of scapegoats whether they were individuals, minority groups or other tribes. The power to divide our communities between *us* and *them*, good and evil, those on God's side and those on Satan's side, became the very power by which our world's systems operate. Had these powers known that in crucifying Jesus they were breaking down every wall of division in which their power lay, they would never have crucified Him.[3]

Five verbs are used in Ephesians 2 to describe what Jesus accomplished. These are: Break down, abolish, murder, create, and reconcile.

> *For he is our peace, who has made us both one and has* **broken down** *the dividing wall, having* **abolished** *in his flesh the hostility, the law of commandments and regulations, so as to* **create** *in himself one new man from the two, thus making peace, and to* **reconcile** *both to God in one body through the cross, having* **put the hostility to death** *(murder) in himself.*[4]

He breaks down the dividing wall.
He abolishes the hostility that was maintained by the law.
He creates a new humanity no longer separated by religious laws.

---

3   1 Corintians. 2:7, Ephesians. 2
4   Ephesians 2:14–16 Mounce

He reconciles both those who were excluded and those who excluded, to God.

He does this by putting to death, or murdering, hostility.

It is the very process of accusation by which we distinguish ourselves and divide the human community into hostile groupings, by which we create sacred laws that serve to strengthen our walls of division, that Jesus comes to annihilate by exposing it.

I see Satan fall like lightning... I see the mythical spiritual creature fall and exposed as being the very earthly empires and structures of power that demand conformity. These powers have promised peace by means of violence and freedom by means of control, but they never have and never will deliver on these promises. The cross exposes the fact that evil finds its most real existence in the violence mankind inflicts on themselves.

The search for being, for sufficiency, has driven humanity to extremes. These conflicting desires could neither be fulfilled nor successfully suppressed. The very laws that prohibited their expression became the means by which they were strengthened. Jesus delivers us from this state of being by bringing us face to face with our true model - the image and likeness of God in human life. Encounter with Him is the transformative event in which our true being is restored. Consequently, the law is fulfilled and abolished simultaneously. It has served its purpose, but has no further function left.

The very way in which we formed our communities, the sense of lack that gave birth to violent rivalry, has lost its basis. From a sense of fullness we are now able to imitate our self-giving heavenly Abba. The implications are practical: Justice needs to be restorative. Unity is not achieved through conformity, but through reconciliation. Reconciliation does not take away the differences, but holds us in relationship while maintaining our differences. That means, differences are no longer a reason for hostility but a reason for celebration.

The enemy is enmity.
The deceiver is deception.
The prince of the power of the air[5] is the spirit, the unseen influence that determines the course of this world. It is the twisted mimetic desire that have kept people bound to their most animalistic survival instincts.

The principalities that did not realize what they were doing,[6] are the very principles by which our civilizations were formed. The Accuser is the accusation. The same principle of accusation that causes chaos in a community also brings order when multiple accusations coalesce[7] and

---

5   Ephesians. 2:2,3
6   1 Corinthians. 2:8
7   come together and form the mass or whole

become focused on a scapegoat. This is *satan* casting out *satan*. The satan is the accusation.

IMPLICATIONS

Mary-Anne and I got married at the young age of 19. A few weeks later we journeyed to Zimbabwe on our first mission trip together. We traveled a number of hours north of Harare where there were remote villages which had never heard the gospel before. These areas did not have any clinics or doctors around and all kinds of sicknesses were evident. It was an extraordinary environment in which to proclaim this beautiful message, knowing that more than human words were needed to benefit this community.

On one particular occasion, we were sleeping in our vehicle next to a group of mud huts belonging to the family of our interpreter. In the morning we were awakened by a commotion. An excited crowd had gathered around our vehicle. One man in particular drew our attention with a smile that seemed to cover his whole face. Our interpreter stumbled out of one of the huts and tried to converse with a crowd who all seemed to speak at once.

They were all from one small village a few miles away. The young man, who was now holding my hand with both his hands, had been a unique part of this village's history.

Our interpreter began to explain: When this 26 year old man was 6 years old, a terrible condition took hold of him. As soon as the sun would set, he became tormented and would howl, cry and scream uncontrollably throughout the night. It obviously disturbed the village and no one was able to get a good night's rest. In their desperation a solution had to be found. (Please remember they did not have the kind of options available to modern communities.)

About a kilometer from the village, a tree was selected and the boy was chained to this tree from sunset to sunrise. The village slept better as the sound of the howling was now muffled.

Our interpreter continued: "*Last night the village brought him to the meeting. He was unusually quiet. After the message, you invited people for prayer. This man came and you prayed with him.*"

My eyes filled with tears as the interpreter concluded: "*Last night was the first night in 20 years that this village slept without the eery howling in the distance. They all overslept!*"

The man holding my hand began to speak excitedly. The interpreter continued: "*He says that he has never slept so well.*"

The reason I told this story - and there are many more - is to make it clear to you, the reader, that I know that torment is real, personal suffering is real and demonic manifestations are real. In no way am I disputing the reality of these experiences. In this chapter I propose a radically new way of understanding this phenomenon. It involves undoing some of the more popular theories of Satan and demons. As I undo these theories, some would prefer to dismiss me as an intellectual theorist who has never experienced the reality of evil. I hope the story above will prompt you to listen a bit longer.

To lose a personal devil is traumatic for those of us who have lived so closely and for so long with this imaginary foe. For some the loss is so great that they find it difficult to continue in a personal relationship with God thereafter! I've heard some say: *Well if Satan is not a person, but a principle, why should we believe in a personal God?* For them the reality of Satan and of God, of good and of evil is so intertwined... so similar, that to lose the one is to lose the other. No! The reality of evil is in no way on the same level as the reality of God. Compared to the substance and person of God, the satan has no substance nor person at all! The existence of God is in no way dependent on the existence of a personal Satan.

THE SATAN IN THE GOSPELS

There is a diversity and progression of thought regarding the satan among the new testament authors. Let's look at some specific examples beginning with the gospel of Matthew and the gospel of John.

> *Then Jesus was led up by the Spirit into the wilderness to be tempted by the devil. And when He had fasted forty days and forty nights, afterward He was hungry. Now when the tempter came to Him, he said, "If You are the Son of God, command that these stones become bread."*

> *But He answered and said, "It is written, 'Man shall not live by bread alone, but by every word that proceeds from the mouth of God.'"*

> *Then the devil took Him up into the holy city, set Him on the pinnacle of the temple, and said to Him, "If You are the Son of God, throw Yourself down. For it is written:*

> *'He shall give His angels charge over you,'*
> *and,*
> *'In their hands they shall bear you up,*
> *Lest you dash your foot against a stone.'"*

> *Jesus said to him, "It is written again, 'You shall not tempt the Lord your God.'"*

> *Again, the devil took Him up on an exceedingly high mountain, and showed Him all the kingdoms of the world and their glory. And he said to Him, "All these things I will give You if You will fall down and worship me."*

Then Jesus said to him, "Away with you, Satan! For it is written, 'You shall worship the Lord your God, and Him only you shall serve.'"

Then the devil left Him, and behold, angels came and ministered to Him.
(Matthew 4:1-11)

All three of these temptations are focused on questioning Jesus' identity and how he will fulfill his vocation.
"What kind of Messiah will you be?"
"What kind of power will you use to fulfill your calling?"
Robert Capon summarizes these temptations as follows:

... the devil pleads (rather convincingly, too) for Jesus to do three altogether sensible things: to use his might to turn stones into bread (and by extension, to do something useful about human hunger); to display his power over death in a well-staged spectacle that would get people's attention; and last and most important, to use the devil's own eminently practical, right-handed [natural force] methods for getting the world to shape up."[8]

Now let us look at John's account of the same temptations. Some of you might have objected already: *"There is no wilderness temptation account in the gospel of John."*

---

8   Kingdom, Grace, Judgment. Robert Capon. Pg 26

Well, yes and no. If the question is whether John tells of a similar account of a 40 day fast and a wilderness experience culminating in an encounter with a personalized devil, then no, John has no such story to tell. But if we frame the question differently... if we ask:

Are there any voices suggesting to Jesus that he should produce miraculous bread?

Is there a temptation to display his supernatural power for the world to see and so prove that he is indeed the long awaited Messiah?

Is there a situation in which the natural powers, the kingdoms of this world, are on offer to him?
The answer to all three of those questions, is "Yes!"

In John 6:13 a large crowd is ready to make him king. The temptation must have been real, for Jesus purposely withdraws to be by himself.

In John 6:30,31 a crowd of people asks him to show them a sign and give them supernatural bread.

In John 7:3-5 his brothers prompt him to go to Jerusalem and perform an open display of his powers, that he might convince the world. (They themselves did not believe.)

So we see that John has the exact same accounts of temptation, but in John's accounts there are no personified devil, these temptations come through people. The fact that the gospel of John has a very different conception of satan and a very different demonology is also evident in the fact that there are no accounts of exorcism in John's gospel. John is beginning to tell a very different story.

POSSESSION

Whenever we have shared these thoughts, the immediate questions that are stirred are in relation to demon possession. Are the gospel accounts of demons and exorcisms simply metaphorical? A simple yes/no answer would not do the question justice. There is no reason why an actual event could not serve to demonstrate deeper (metaphorical) meaning. So, yes, there certainly is more to the stories than historical accounts of actual events. Similarly, recognizing the truth these stories wanted to communicate does not mean that there were no actual events. Each instance needs to be evaluated on its own merit.

I have witnessed the phenomenon of what is known in Christian circles as demon possession. The phenomenon is real. How we explain this phenomenon, however, needs to progress beyond the magical and mythical language we have used in religious environments.

Human beings, created in the image and likeness of God, have creative capacities which have often been underestimated. We are able to separate certain ideas and qualities from ourselves and project them, or externalize them. This is, in a way, an act of creation. Sometimes we project these qualities onto others - often without any real basis. But the very expectation to see certain qualities in another person creates an environment in which it becomes not only possible, but likely for those qualities to manifest. Our expectations of others, good or bad, awaken those possibilities in others.

In other instances, we project our ideas onto imagined entities. The fact that we imagined them does not mean that they have no influence. A monster under your child's bed might have no real existence for you, but it can be real enough for the child to cause actual torment. What would happen if you became as convinced about the monster's existence as your child? What would happen if your whole church agreed that there is indeed a demonic monster under that bed? Can you imagine the prayer meetings in which sincere believers would battle with this force, have arguments with it and discover the means by which it found entrance into the house? Such attention would energize this image to such an extent that it would take on a form of reality. Would your child still be able to sleep in that room?

This is admittedly an oversimplified example. The point is that we are able to create and energize images to the extent that they have real influence.

Raymund Schwager gives the following insight:

> *As collective projections and accusations are extremely powerful, they affect their victims deeply from within. The possessed are those who submit to a collective accusation in the name of an otherworldly power, who experience a total inward breakdown, and who completely internalize the evil judgement that others make about them. Victims such as these no longer exercise their own judgement and have no will of their own, for the collective projection in which they believe controls them as an alien will and commands them what to do. This projection is the work of many, so for the possessed the number of demons is often legion (Mark 5:1-20).[9]*

Jean-Michel Oughourlian gives multiple examples of the mechanism of possession in his book, *Puppets of Desire.* Of particular interest is the way in which desires can take on personality. If *self* is formed by desire, then different desires can form different personalities. For those who are interested in the topic of possession, this is a great resource. The purpose of this chapter is not to give a comprehensive

---

9   Raymund Schwager, Banished from Eden, pg 152

explanation of possession but simply to introduce an alternative understanding of it within the mimetic context.

The bottom line is this: There is not one act of stealing, one act of abuse, one act of murder, committed in this world by supernatural naughty little fallen angels. They are all committed by human beings whose desires have been perverted and whose minds have been messed up.

Such evil can be greatly intensified when whole communities participate in a perverted mimetic cycle. When we witness the outrageous brutality of Isis or remember the scale and depravity of violence committed by Hitler and his Nazis, evil becomes overwhelming. Such an overwhelming sense of evil makes it easy to imagine a single personality behind it all. The scriptures, however, progressively expose the structure of evil as a purely human phenomenon.

FIGHTING EVIL

So how do we fight this evil?

Becoming aware of the environments, processes and cycles in which fear functions and twists our desires to become harmful, opens up new possibilities of dealing with this evil.

Let's look at how to resist evil in three areas: Our personal relationships, in the context of national interests, and finally in the context of a diversity of religions.

Recognizing how projections (often unjustified) and counter projections only serve to energize the movements that cause conflict, is an essential first step to stopping this cycle.

In a situation of conflict, or even just irritation, it can be enlightening to ask: "What is it in me that causes this irritation?" A person's words, actions, or simply their presence might repel us. Instead of just focusing on how irritating the person is, we can recognize that accusation always says something about ourselves as well. Instead of projecting all we cannot bear to see in ourselves, onto the *other* evil person, we can begin to perceive our own contribution to the conflict. This also opens the opportunity to acknowledge the beauty and value of the other person. In short, evil is not located in any one person; it is a possibility within the mimetic cycle, a latent energy within the relational movements between us.

In the same way as individuals expel their own inner evils by projecting them onto others, communities have preserved their inner unity by means of the scapegoating mechanism. Similarly nations have preserved their order by projecting evil beyond their borders and in the process have demonized other nations and cultures. Nationalistic and patriotic feelings are ideal environments in which to breed callousness towards the suffering of others who do not fall within the borders of our concern.

If Jesus means anything to us, if His message has any value, then the central focus of what he accomplished - the breaking down of dividing walls, the abolishing of hostility, the reconciliation of different people groups - should at least make us cautious of blind patriotic sentiment. How do we reach beyond our borders and alleviate the suffering of others? How many of the borders we created are justified in the light of reconciliation? In the same way as personal conflict does not always mean that I am right and the other is wrong, my nation might not always be right either. Resist evil by being the conscience of your culture, by testifying to the truth within your nation even when its labeled as unpatriotic.

Lastly, the demonization of other religions is probably the easiest to do and the most difficult to eradicate. Resist it! The God who is the source of all existence, has no insecurity issues. You are free to acknowledge what is beautiful and true in any religion. This by no means implies that all religions are the same, but that we are able to recognize the distinctions and the similarities and appreciate them all. What remains evil, no matter what religious title it bears, is violating and harming Gods creation.

Resist evil by recognizing and exposing "sacred" violence within your own religion. Resist evil, by recognizing the beauty within other religions and developing meaningful relationships with those of different faiths.

In so doing you will be following in the footsteps of the author of our faith, the one who broke down dividing walls and brought enmity between different religious groupings to an end. You will be emulating the one who is creative in reconciliation and opposed only to opposition itself.

15 - ATONEMENT THEORIES AND SACRIFICE

Salvation and sacrifice have always been closely associated. And it is no wonder, for the sacred violence against a single victim saved each member of the community from becoming victims of senseless violence.

Jesus came, not to endorse the magical thinking that emerged from the practice of sacrifice, but to expose these hidden realities. The salvation he brings is therefore very different from the ideas of salvation that are so deeply buried in human history and consciousness.

In this chapter we'll consider three atonement theories and how they relate to sacrifice. In considering these questions we'll look in particular at the role of sacrifice within each of these theories. In addition, each of these theologies will be placed in the context of mimetic theory, evaluating both the enhancements and contradictions created by this context.

1. CHRISTUS VICTOR

SUMMARY

The main emphasis of the *Christus Victor* view is Christ's victory over evil, exemplified by this verse: "*The Son of God was revealed for this purpose: to destroy the Devil's works*" (1 John 3:8 HCSB).

The world has been taken captive by the prince of this world. Mankind has been trapped and brought into slavery to do his will. Christ comes to judge the prince of this world, to liberate us from this kingdom of darkness, and free us from the fear of death and the rule of sin.

HISTORY

This victory motif is one of the most ancient views. It was discussed by a variety of early Christian thinkers. In these early discussions Christ was sometimes seen as part of an exchange with the devil. God offered Jesus to Satan as the ransom price for humanity.

Other variations focused on the fact that Satan did not know what he was doing in murdering Christ. "*None of the rulers of this age knew this wisdom, for if they had known it, they would not have crucified the Lord of glory.*"[1] As death swallowed up Jesus, it soon became apparent that it swallowed more than it could "stomach", and so spewed Christ out, just as the big fish had to spew out Jonah.

---

1   1 Corinthians 2:8–9 HCSB

Many such creative examples were used to portray God's victory over Satan. However, when these metaphors are pushed too far in a literal sense, cracks appear.

Why does God have to negotiate with Satan?

What right does Satan have?

Was God acting deceptively in snaring Satan into this trap?

Is military and battle imagery the best way to understand Christ's mission?

Such questions, and the inadequate answers that were offered, eventually caused this theme to fade and other models to emerge. Modern scholars have however, revisited the Christus Victor model and provided more sound explanations of this theme.[2] There is undoubtedly much biblical support for it.

Walter Wink, in his book, *Engaging the Powers*, proposes an interesting reason for why this classic theology lost favor:

> *The Christus Victor theology fell out of favor, not because of intrinsic inadequacies, but because it was subversive to the churches' role as a state religion. The church no longer saw the demonic as lodged in the empire, but in the empire's enemies. Atonement became a highly individualized transaction between the believer and God; society was assumed to be Christian, so the idea that the*

---

2   The nature of Atonement: Four views;
Healing the Gospel, by Derek Flood;
Atonement, Justice and Peace by Darrin W. Snyder

work of Christ entails the radical critique of society was largely abandoned.

I agree with Walter that the state religion had good reasons to challenge the Christus Victor view, however, there were also real, intrinsic inadequacies as we'll see shortly.

SCRIPTURAL BASIS

Underlying the Christus Victor model is an apocalyptic worldview. In a world torn between good and evil, a world plagued by chaos because of the battle between God's forces and the enemy's forces, an expectation developed for a final battle in which God would once and for all subdue his enemies. The expectation that history has a forward motion towards a conclusive end provided the death and resurrection of Jesus with cosmic significance.

According to the gospel of John, Jesus understood his mission as a confrontation with, and judgment of, the prince of this world. *"Now is the judgment of this world: now shall the prince of this world be cast out."*[3]

This prince, also known as the devil, has trapped people and taken them captive to do his will (2 Timothy 2:26). Paul refers to it as slavery to the elemental forces of the world (Galatians 4:3) and as slavery to sin (Romans 6:17). In spite of Paul's best religious efforts to free himself, he comes to a

---

3   John 12:31 KJV, see also John 16:11

place of total desperation: "*O wretched man that I am, who will rescue me...*" (Rom 7:24)

It is in the midst of this battle that Jesus Christ arrives (Romans 7:25) and wins the battle for us, setting us free. "*...it is for freedom that Christ has set you free...*"[4] He does this through the foolishness of the cross. The principalities and powers had no idea what they were participating in (1 Corintians2:8). They thought that a great victory was being won as they nailed Christ to that cross, but all the while God was nailing the very system they relied on to that cross and in so doing was stripping them of their power (Colossians 2:14,15).

Christus Victor also contains a theme of ongoing battle. Because the enemy is conquered and we are liberated, we need not go back to a place of enslavement again... but it is possible to do just that. Evil continues to be a present reality (Galatians 1:4) and the world's system of enslavement remains under the sway of the evil one (1 John 5:19). Consequently there is an ongoing battle (Ephesians 6:12), but it is decidedly different. Exactly how it differs, though, can be difficult to explain in the context of the Christus Victor view as we'll shortly discover.

---

4   Gal 5:1

SACRIFICIAL INTERPRETATION

Mark Heim so beautifully uses the Narnia story to illustrate the subversion of sacrifice and defeat of enemy powers. Edmond, who through his betrayal has joined the enemy forces, is heading towards a sacrificial death.

He is rescued at the last minute, and returns to fight on the side of the Christ-lion Aslan. But the evil powers under a flag of truce insist that Edmund must be handed over to them, that there must be retribution for every treachery, death for death. The Christ-lion Aslan agrees to be handed over and killed in Edmund's place, on the condition that the evil powers renounce their claim on his life. This law of retribution and the sacrificial process of exchange based on it (in which an innocent one may die on behalf of others and so protect them) are known to all from the earliest times. It is called "Deep Magic from the Dawn of Time." This has been going on for ages. There is an ancient stone altar on which Edmund was to be killed, and upon which Aslan is actually sacrificed. The act has a mysterious, sacred aura and an air of inevitability. The evil powers love this arrangement and, incidentally, have no intention of keeping their bargain. Once Aslan is dead, they intend to kill also those he meant to save. This treachery is a key point, because it tips off the reader that this exchange itself cannot be the final word, nor the substance of the divine plan. It is a decidedly lower magic.

The resurrection comes into this story as an unexpected development, from what the book calls "Deeper Magic from Before the Dawn of Time," something about which the evil powers know nothing. The violent mystery of sacrifice goes back to the dawn of our human time. But it has no purchase in the original blessing of creation that stands even further back still. And when Aslan rises from the dead, the ancient stone altar on which the sacrifice was offered cracks and crumbles in pieces, never to be used again. The substitution of Aslan for Edmund cannot save if it is simply a variation on the same sacrificial theme rather than an act to overthrow that process altogether. The stained stone may have been the centerpiece of religion and sacred awe in human history. But it was not God's altar. The gospel is not ultimately about exchange of victims, but about ending the bloodshed.[5]

Battle and violent imagery are prevalent in the Chritus Victor atonement theory and might well be one of the reasons it fell out of favor. However, the violence is not committed by God against humanity, or worse, by the Father against his son, but rather, the battle is against the forces of darkness. In this sense the sacrificial aspect of this view does not suffer from the mythical influences of an angry God who needs to be appeased. Rather, the sacrifice of Christ is a supreme act of love in which he sacrifices

5   Mark S. Heim. *Saved from Sacrifice: A Theology of the Cross* (Kindle Locations 2715-2729). Kindle Edition.

himself to free us from the dominion of evil. Its sacrificial interpretation is therefore one of radical subversion.

LIMITATIONS

Early interpretors often pushed the metaphors too far. (Not much has changed!) In doing so they had to explain how God deceived Satan, yet remained a God of truth. A personified Satan legitimately raised questions regarding his rights: Did Satan have rights to humanity to the extent that God had to ransom us from Satan?

A defeated and personified Satan also causes difficulties with understanding the ongoing evil in this world. If an individual personality, Satan, is the ultimate source of evil, and if he was utterly defeated, why does evil continue to prosper in this world?

CHRISTUS VICTOR IN THE CONTEXT OF MIMETIC THEORY

Mimetic realism is not concerned with an individual or personalized Satan, but rather with *the satan*, the accusation and the deception that produces innocent victims in our world. As such, it is not encumbered with having to explain interpersonal relations between God and a personified Satan. God is not actively trying to deceive anyone, but He orchestrates a situation in which deception itself will be exposed for what it really is. Neither is the ransom a payment to a third party that somehow has rights to such a payment, rather it is simply the price that needed to be paid for our eyes to be opened to recognize the true character of God, man and evil.

Victory over evil and healing from our demonic visions of God are therefore inseparably bound. The one cannot happen without the other - the same light that dispels the nothingness of darkness is the light that allows us to see a God that values us above all else.

The enormous scope of salvation is also very well served by a deep understanding of human history inherent in Mimetic Theory. A thorough anthropological view of salvation liberates it from a purely religious arena, in which our spiritual language makes it irrelevant to actual life. As Jesus retells the human story, we discover a God deeply aware, even partaking of our chaotic human lives. He does not speak in magical heavenly riddles, but He speaks as a man, from a human point of view. The sociological foundations of our civilizations, the principalities and powers, are exposed. But more than that... Paul sees even the reconciliation of principalities and powers![6] This gospel can transform our societies, and rebuild our foundations. The scope is therefore much larger than our individual decisions to make Jesus Lord of our lives. Rather, Paul declares that in Christ he finds a vision that changes the way he sees every person; in fact it changes the way he sees

6   Colossians 1:16-20

all of creation.[7] This message inspires faith-communities that resist evil, break down walls of discrimination, and in so doing they manifest God's kingdom of light right here and right now on this earth. God sees nothing less than the reconciliation of all things in which He is Lord of all.

2. MORAL INFLUENCE/EXAMPLE THEORY

SUMMARY

Within the Moral Example Theory, Jesus is the perfect example of what it means to be human. God tried to show and teach us throughout human history and specifically through the Law and prophets, but we failed to understand or live up to that standard. And so God sent his Son to show us what life, as he intended it, looks like. In doing so, God's intention is to transform human communities through the example of what true love and justice is. Much emphasis is therefore placed on the life and teaching of Jesus.

HISTORY

This viewpoint probably predates even the Christus Victor view. It is certainly one of the first to be committed to writing. Clement of Alexandria (150-215 AC) wrote:

> *For [Christ] came down, for this he assumed human nature, for this he willingly endured the sufferings of humanity, that he being reduced to the measure of our weakness, he might raise us to the measure of his power.*

7   2 Corintians 5:18

> *And just before he poured out his offering, when he gave himself as ransom, he left us a new testament: "I give you my love." What is the nature and extent of this love? For each of us he laid down his life, the life which was worth the whole universe, and he requires in return that we should do the same for each other.* [8]

A number of early church Fathers spoke of the exemplary life of Christ. The theory was later developed more fully by Peter Abelard (1079 - 1142), a French abbot, theologian and philosopher. It continues to be a popular perspective, but has mostly been demoted to a secondary status, as a complimentary view to one of the other atonement theories.

Scriptural Basis

"Follow me" must be the clearest scriptural imperative from the mouth of Jesus himself. A number of scriptures also point to Jesus following the example of his Father. Jesus admonishes his followers to do the same. After teaching about the extravagant generosity of his Father, even towards those opposed to him, he says: "*You therefore must be perfect (fully realized, complete), as your heavenly Father is perfect*" (Matthew 5:48). Paul echoes the same message: "*Therefore be imitators of God, as beloved children. And walk in love, as Christ loved us and gave himself up for us, a fragrant offering and sacrifice to God*" (Ephesians 5:1,2).

---

8   Clement, Quis Dives Salvetur 37 in Clement of Alexandria: The Exhortation to the Greeks, ed. G. W. Butterworth, Cambridge: Loeb Classical Library, Harvard University Press, 1960, 346

The night before his crucifixion, Jesus washes his disciples feet and says: "*If I then, your Lord and Teacher, have washed your feet, you also ought to wash one another's feet*" (John 13:14).

The whole purpose of Jesus' coming is to bring about a kingdom that is the inverse of so many aspects of human societies: The servant is the greatest. The least is the most important. A world in which evil is not repaid with evil, but forgiveness is the only revenge.

Sacrificial Interpretation

This view has none of the demonology necessary for the Christus Victor theory. Neither does the vengeful God of myth make an appearance.

Moral Influence Theory does not see the cross as the satisfaction of God's vengeance, but rather as the satisfaction of his love. It is the ultimate self giving. "*Greater love has no one than this, that someone lay down his life for his friends*" (John 15:13).

Limitations

Those opposed to this view argue that if Jesus was a mere example for us, then how does he differ from other great men and woman who have laid down their lives in service of others?

Maybe the criticism has to do with the unfortunate choice of words to describe the theory. 'Moral' is mainly associated with behavior. Consequently, the depth of our mimetic connection is not well communicated by the word 'moral'.

MORAL INFLUENCE IN THE CONTEXT OF MIMETIC THEORY

There might be much more to the Moral Influence Atonement Theory than what was initially perceived. The discovery of mirror neurons and advances in psychology demonstrate how deeply mimetic we are. Mimetic Theory further illustrates how the human capacity to reflect has been an integral part of how our cultures and civilizations have formed and developed. To find a model worthy of reflecting would have implications for every aspect of society. The concern raised that according to the Moral Influence Theory any good person can be a model and therefore it reduces the uniqueness of Jesus Christ, is also unfounded. It is precisely because Christ recapitulates all of human history, in a way that no other model has ever done, that it makes him such a unique model.

3. PENAL SUBSTITUTION OR SATISFACTION THEORY
SUMMARY:

The Penal Substitution view can be stated as follows:
The sin of mankind has offended God's honor and justice and so has caused broken relationship between us and God, between one another, and within creation. Only

through the just penalty or punishment of sin can the honor of God be restored. Mankind, however, was unable to pay this price. God, despite his offense, still loved us and therefore sent his son to pay this price in our stead, or as our substitute. The price that satisfies God's offense is nothing less than the blood of his own innocent son.

HISTORY

Anselm of Canterbury is considered the first to begin the development of this view in his 1098 publication, 'Cur Deus Homo'. The theory continued to be developed within a legal and penal framework by later theologians including Luther and Calvin.

Anselm identified some of the inadequacies with the Christus Victor view, explicitly rejecting the idea that Satan had rights that had to be satisfied with a ransom payment. But there were other factors that influenced Anselm as well.

Anselm lived in a very hierarchical society in which different classes were due different degrees of honor. To offend a peasant did not cost one as much, if anything, as offending a landlord. Offending the king however, could quite literally cost you your life! And so, an offense was measured not solely by the nature of the deed, but by whom it offended. It was also during this time that the penitential system was developing.

Anselm's satisfaction atonement image likely originated as a reflection of the penitential system and the sacrament of private penance that was developing throughout the medieval era and also reflected the feudal lord who gave protection to his vassals but also exacted penalties for offenses against his honor.[9]

Scriptural Basis

Penal Substitution Theory (PST) assumes very specific meanings for sin, justice and the sacrifice of Christ. We'll consider each of these.

- The sinfulness and guilt of humanity.

Supporters of Satisfaction Theory often pride themselves in taking sin seriously, quoting Anselm: "*We have yet to measure the gravity of sin.*"

All of humanity without exception are sinful and guilty (Romans 3:23). No matter how small or infrequent one's sin is, the guilt and the penalty due remain the same, namely death (Romans 6:23, James 2:10). The only way to avoid this grave penalty is to give God perfect obedience. But no one ever has or ever could satisfy this requirement (Eccl. 7:20, Job 15:14, Romans 5).

---

9   J. Denny Weaver. The Nonviolent Atonement, Second Edition (Kindle Locations 282-285). Kindle Edition.

This condition of total depravity is not simply due to personal wrongdoings, but a condition we are born into as David laments (Psalm 51:5).

In defining PST, Thomas R. Schreiner, describes sin and the penalty due to sin as follows:

> *Sinners deserve eternal punishment in hell from God himself because of their sin and guilt. God's holy anger is directed (Rom 1:18) against all those who have sinned and fall short of the glory of God (Rom 3:23). And yet because of God's great love, he sent Christ to bear the punishment of our sins. Christ died in our place, took to himself our sin (2 Cor 5:21) and guilt (Gal 3:10), and bore our penalty so that we might receive forgiveness of sins.*[10]

- The holiness of God and retributive justice.

According to this view, the holiness of God is offended at every sin and demands that reparations be paid to appease him and make forgiveness possible. Justice, within PST, takes on a very definite form, namely, retributive justice. If God is just, then everyone needs to get what they deserve, either reward or punishment. And the punishment needs to be equal to the sin. As the theory of penal substitution developed this concept of retributive justice became the very attribute that defined God.

---

10   The Nature of Atonement, (Kindle location 775) Kindle Edition

SACRIFICIAL INTERPRETATION

PST understands sacrifice as the penalty of death demanded by a just (justly offended) God in order to satisfy his honor. In this regard PST adopts most of the magical qualities of sacrifice that are present in myth. It knows nothing of the horror of sacrifice, or its murderous origins. An angry God's demand for blood is at its center. Despite the more legal terminology in which the theory was developed, the reality is savage: God's revenge is only satisfied by the magical blood of those who offended him... or by a suitable substitute.

LIMITATIONS

- Terminology

The words 'substitution' or 'penal' are not used in the new testament. These are interpretations, superimposed on phrases such as: "*Christ died for us*". The "*for*" has been interpreted as substitutionary, and the death Christ "*died*" has been interpreted as punishment. However, there are other ways of interpreting these phrases. The "*for*" can also be interpreted as representative. In other words, Christ died as our representative, not as our substitute.

When Caiaphas said: "*its better for one man to die for the nation, than for the whole nation to perish*" (John 11:45–46) he conveys a typical substitutionary understanding. One dies so that the nation may live. However, Paul understands the death of Christ very differently when he writes: "*if *one has died for all, then all have died*" (2 Cor 5:14). This conveys a representative understanding. One dies as the representative of all, therefore all have died.

Similarly, Christ's death can be seen as his ultimate gift of love to deliver us from our illusions. It is not necessarily God's punishment (as advocated by PST) that causes his death, but rather, our violence that murders him.

- Central Message

The greatest weakness of PST, I believe, is its central message: Jesus came to save us from an angry God. One can whitewash the message and decorate it with kind and loving words, but its basic message remains one of revenge: God's justice needs to be satisfied and the only way to accomplish that is through violence and the spilling of blood!

- Retributive Justice

The concept of substitution is then used to make an argument for God's love. Although He can rightly demand our blood, He lovingly provides the blood of his innocent son. However, love is not central to what this theory has to say about the nature and character of God, retributive justice is. The substitution is only provided because justice demands blood. Love is simply doing its best to preserve life under the dominion of retributive justice.

- Redemptive Violence

The effect of a God who accomplishes redemption through retributive justice is that the myth of redemptive violence remains central. God overcomes evil by means of violence. Violence is therefore not condemned but once again glorified as the method by which chaos is transformed into order and enemies are conquered. The very quality that most accurately portrays evil, is honored as the quality that saves us from evil.

- Forgiveness

The role of forgiveness is not clear in a system where the debt is paid in full. Why is forgiveness necessary if the exact price has been paid and full reparation has been made? The forgiveness presented by PST seems little more than a sentimental gesture made after the real work of retributive justice.

- Resurrection is Arbitrary

Based on the presumption that the death of Jesus is the required payment for sin, the logical conclusion is that his death dealt with the sin problem. The resurrection, therefore, becomes an afterthought in the drama of salvation. The problem with that argument is that Paul sees, not the death, but the resurrection as the definitive event that saves: "*if Christ is not risen, your faith is futile; you are still in your sins!*" (1 Corinthians 15:17). In other words, his death did not solve the sin problem - his resurrection did.

The logic of most PST messages preached, arguments made and books written would remain perfectly in tact if one removed every reference to the resurrection from them!

PST IN THE CONTEXT OF MIMETIC THEORY

In sacrificial myths, the victim is often portrayed as guilty and the crowd as innocent. PST does progress from this view by acknowledging the guilt of the crowd. It is the guilt of the crowd transferred to the sacrifice that justifies the violence done to the sacrificial victim. However, PST seems ignorant of what the crowd is guilty of, namely, violence that escalates into murder disguised as sacrifice.

Within PST sin is defined as any disobedience to God and is measured by the offense it causes God. I believe the mimetic model gives us a much clearer definition of sin and is discussed in detail in the next chapter. In summary, the most obvious manifestation of sin is violence. Violence does not always lead to murder, but violence is always destructive and causes suffering. As such, words that break down are violent, unjust laws are a violation of people's freedom, etc.

In this sense, Jesus does suffer the punishment for our sins, but in a decidedly different way than PST would argue. This is not a punishment demanded by a just God or given by an offended Father. Rather he suffers the consequences of our injustice, is beaten by our wickedness, and bruised by our iniquity. He bore the brunt of a perverted and twisted generation, formed by a perverted mimetic cycle, and as such he suffered the penalty or consequences of our sin with us.

SUMMARY

We have done a quick overview of three prominent atonement theories. In addition we have looked at how Mimetic Theory can enrich these and in some cases critique these atonement theories. The purpose of this was simply to provide background information for what is about to be presented in Chapter 16, *Mimetic At-One-Ment*.

16 - MIMETIC AT-ONE-MENT

What privilege language affords us. We are able to communicate ideas, build upon them and reconfigure them. We have looked at the history of some of the greatest ideas - ideas about sacrifice, God, the satan and the Messiah. In addition, some of the most influential modern ideas namely, Mimetic Theory, have been added to the mix. In the previous chapter we examined how these ideas have been used to develop theories of atonement.

In a way, this chapter is the simple conclusion of all the complex concepts that were discussed before. What I will attempt to do now, is to take all we have examined so far and starting from the most basic assumptions, build a vision of atonement that uses both ancient insights and modern understanding of the nature of man and our environment. I will call this vision, *Mimetic Atonement*, or *Reflective Atonement*. The name Mimetic Atonement, as I use it here, does not simply refer to the inclusion of Mimetic Theory into a theory of atonement. It does that, but more. It is specifically the reflective or revelatory meanings attached to "mimetic" that are significant and central to this idea of Mimetic Atonement.

SUMMARY

Humans are by nature reflective and as such we cannot be our true selves if we do not have a reference for what true humanity is. We reflect the God we perceive (Genesis 1:26). A distortion of this reflection is an evil that affects everything: our view of the divine, of ourselves, of one another and of creation. The implications are both personal and social, for our concepts find expression in social structures of power. Jesus comes as *the true light that enlightens every man* (John 1:9), *to give us understanding, that we may know the true One, and we are in him who is true* (1 John 5:20), as the living demonstration of who God really is and therefore who we really are as His image and likeness.

The most fundamental, rudimentary identity is the self-of-desire. If God's desire for us is not the source of our reflection, we are no longer truly ourselves. Direct encounter with him is replaced by a mediated encounter with our projections of him. Consequently, Jesus comes to correct the most basic fault - no one has seen the Father, no one has their true model in sight. "*Until this moment God remained invisible to man; now the authentic, incarnate begotten son, the blueprint of mankind's design who represents the innermost being of God, the son who is*

296

in the bosom of the father, brings him into full view! He is the official authority qualified to announce God! He is our guide who accurately declares and interprets the invisible God within us."[1] In encounter with him, we are transformed (2 Corinthians 3:18) as we see again the authentic desire that gave us birth and we are transferred from a kingdom of darkness into a kingdom of light. The deceptions that formed us are exposed and our true selves emerge. Again, the implications are both personal and social as the very principalities and powers of this world are reconciled to the mind of Christ. It is nothing less than a whole new creation in which all things are of God (2 Corinthians 5:18).

THE PROBLEM

It is useful to think of atonement as at-one-ment. It speaks of a mending of relationship, a restored unity. But why did it need mending? The traditional answer includes the concept of original sin, and for most people that means that somebody, somewhere, long ago messed up, and that is why we have so many troubles.

It might be a surprise to some that the Old Testament has no developed doctrine of original sin. Whenever the prophets and scribes speak about the condition of humanity and the sin that plagues them, they never point to the story of Adam and Eve as the reason for our suffering; they don't theorize about original sin. They simply point to the

---

1   John 1:18 The Mirror Bible

jealousy, the injustice and the violence that is presently happening and warn people to stop it.

The concept of original sin only comes into being after the resurrection! Mankind is faced with a salvation so large, that for the first time we are able to see the enormity of the problem we were caught in.

Jesus came to heal humanity of a blindness we were born with - the enormity of our error only became evident post enlightenment. A man born blind has no memory of what it was like to see. The extent to which he cannot function normally, the extent of his blindness, will only be fully known after he has been healed. It is when he experiences restored sight that he fully realizes what it meant to be blind!

The salvation Jesus accomplishes is a solution so great that we only realize the enormity of the problem after we experience this salvation. The concept of original sin therefore first appeared after the resurrection. Paul offered many creative interpretations of scripture as he sought to find words and metaphors large enough to do justice to this overwhelming gospel. The significance of the singular event of Christ, the way in which it compressed all time and brought about a new kind of time, the much greater reality of a whole new creation, cried out for a new way of understanding the problem as well. The problem which he now saw, was larger than what he ever imagined. No wonder laws and regulations could not solve the problem - they did not even understand the problem.

What drove Paul to see that Jew and Gentile now constitute one people of God was not his own imagination or sense of social justice, and it certainly was not his "straight" reading of his Bible. If anything, putting Jew and non-Jew on the same level cuts against the Old Testament grain. What drove Paul to this revolutionary, countercultural conclusion was the reality of the resurrection of Christ. As Sanders and others have argued, Paul's theology— in Romans 5: 12- 21 and everywhere else— began with the reorienting reality of the risen Christ. That was his point of departure, the center around which everything else now revolved— the hermeneutical focal point around which Paul's own Scripture was now to be reinterpreted... The crucified and risen Son of God was God's climactic, fundamentally drastic, and unexpected act of salvation. For God to have provided a "solution" of such earth-shattering significance, there must have been a corresponding "problem" it was designed to address. God's solution through the death and resurrection of Jesus exposed the true plight of humanity. Because of the nature of the solution, Paul came to understand that the human

*plight was far deeper and more widespread than his own
Jewish worldview thought.*[2]

In Romans 5 Paul finds a picture in Adam that begins to
show the importance of the event and person of Christ.
But even in finding a picture somewhat similar, Paul
immediately makes it clear that the comparison is actually
still out of proportion! What is similar is this: An event in
our prehistoric past, symbolized by Adam's disobedience,
had enormous consequences for all of humanity thereafter.
Such a cataclysmic event has occurred once again. God has
broken into our history and through this event realized a
new possibility for humanity. The resurrection opens up a
whole new way of being human.

And so Paul is one of the first theologians that sees and tries
to describe the depth and origin of the human problem. It
goes much deeper than wrong conduct - that's only the end
result of a process that needs to change. What energizes
this underlying process? It goes even deeper than wrong
belief! It has to do with the origin of our desires, with the
processes that formed us. It is a blindness that has its origin
in the very dawn of humanity... the very events that made
us human.

2   Enns, Peter (2012-01-01). The Evolution of Adam, What
the Bible Does and Doesn't Say about Human Origins (p. 131). Baker
Publishing Group. Kindle Edition.

The sin of humanity is an error so intrinsic to the history that formed us, so pervasive, that we are unable to recognize it by ourselves. It is the very process that formed our consciousness and as such remained hidden from conscious awareness. It is an error of which we are oblivious and so we only strengthen the error by claiming to know what is wrong. We were born blind, or as Jesus put it: we tried to remove the speck from our brother's eye, not recognizing the beam in our own. This does not mean that we are naturally evil! We are naturally able to realize many possibilities of being - the fact is that the wrong possibility was realized.

For a reflective being that can be whatever it beholds, the possibilities of being are infinite. The process of reflection includes various forms of interpretation by which the image can be deformed. The Genesis story sees the ultimate being of man as a reflection of the creative self-giving God. However, another possibility was present at the very beginning of the human race, symbolized by the tree of the knowledge of good and evil.

Sin began as we misread the intentions of God (Genesis 3) and so constructed a god-of-our-confusion, which became the model of our twisted desires (James 1) and the birthplace of a *self* not recognized by God. We thus alienated ourselves from the true One and from our true selves, which is only to be found in our true origin - the God who adores us. The implications are not only personal or individual, but they result in a world filled with tormented communities, kept in bondage to perverted desire.

> *What is the source of wars and fights among you? Don't they come from the cravings that are at war within you? You desire and do not have. You murder and covet and cannot obtain. You fight and war. You do not have because you do not ask. You ask and don't receive because you ask with wrong motives, so that you may spend it on your evil desires.*
> (James 4:1–3 HCSB)

The question of original sin is therefore not one of finding yet another scapegoat, yet another entity to blame for our condition. The question is not, how did Adam's sin affect us, but rather how does the forgiveness of Christ affect Adam.

Adam is our history, Christ is our future, for Christ has opened up a whole new way of being human.

Salvation is therefore nothing less than the undoing of the self-of-desire, in order to introduce us again to the authentic desire that gave us birth and so to reconstruct a true-self-of-true-desire (James 1:23).

This encounter is both destructive and restorative.

It is destructive in that it is the event in which the satan, the accusation, the deception is exposed and in this exposing act, it is defeated. It is destructive in that the self-of-false-desire is undone and brought to naught.

I love the poetic interpretation of James 1:22-25 in the Mirror translation:

Give the word your undivided attention; do not underestimate yourself. Make the calculation. There can only be one logical conclusion: your authentic origin is mirrored in the word. You are God's poem; let his voice make poetry of your life! The difference between a mere spectator and a participator is that both of them hear the same voice and perceive in its message the face of their own genesis reflected as in a mirror; they realize that they are looking at themselves, but for the one it seems just too good to be true, he departs (back to his old way of seeing himself) never giving another thought to the man he saw there in the mirror. The other one is mesmerized by what he sees; he is captivated by the effect of a law that frees man from the obligation to the old written code that restricted him to his own efforts and willpower. No distraction or contradiction can dim the impact of what he sees in that mirror concerning the law of perfect liberty that now frees him to get on with the act of living the life.[3]

---

3   Du Toit, Francois (2012-07-02). Mirror Bible (Kindle Locations 6533-6549). Mirror Word Publishing. Kindle Edition.

"*...perceive in its message the face of their own genesis.*" This encounter is a restorative event in that we see the face of our beginning and so the true-self-of-authentic-desire is redeemed and healed. Christ is therefore both the Victor and the ultimate Model simultaneously. As such, Mimetic At-one-ment incorporates the best of Christus Victor and Moral Influence theories. At the same time it rejects much of the mythical understanding of sacrifice as incorporated in the Penal Substitution Theory.

SIN AND EVIL

Sin and evil are naturally connected concepts. Sin is participating in evil... it is what makes evil, human. Remember, evil is experienced most acutely when the intensity of suffering coincides with the intent to cause harm. Consequently, sin is both the perverted intention and the resultant actions that cause suffering, either to yourself, to others, or to creation.

Misinterpreting the intention or desire of God is the most elemental mistake humanity has made according to the Genesis 3 story. It is the event in which we lose clear sight of who God is and, in our confusion, unconsciously look at one another to energize our desires. Significantly, the source of twisted desire is lack, not fullness; it's the perception that God withholds something from us. The nature of this sense of lack is not only a lack of possession (the fruit), but a lack of being (being like God). This perverted model is the basis

304

for acts of sin. Lying, stealing, violence all proceed from imitating/mirroring the desires of the wrong model, or a good model wrongly perceived. This misconception of God also gives birth to many of our myths, rituals and religions.

The scope of this twisted mimetic cycle is enormous. Sin is much more than a personal moral failing, although it may include that. The twisted desires we reflect personally cannot but become an integral part of our communities. The gravity of sin is indeed staggering if we consider that we have built our civilizations upon the myth of redemptive violence. Reconciliation, therefore, includes the transformation of the principalities and powers, the very thought structures that form our social structures. Obviously individuals need healing, but our societies need healing too if individual healing is to be sustained.

CONSEQUENCES OF SIN AND PUNISHMENT

The consequence of sin is suffering to both the perpetrator and the victim. The perpetrator, however, incurs guilt. Therefore, the suffering that a perpetrator experiences is often interpreted as punishment. In a sense this is true, but we need to clarify this point. No third party, including God, has to intervene to cause the consequences of sin - it happens naturally.

There is another kind of punishment. It is the kind of discipline a father gives a child. It is direct and personal.

The aim of this kind of punishment is not retribution, but guidance and restoration.

CONSEQUENCES OF SIN AND BROKEN RELATIONSHIP

Within the Penal Substitutionary Theory, sin caused an offense within God and consequently, he withdrew from sinful man. Atonement in this context is therefore concerned with satisfying God's offense or sense of justice.

In Mimetic Atonement, the problem begins with mankind misinterpreting the intentions of God. As such it is not God who withdraws from mankind. Rather, we withdraw, both from God and from our true selves. In turning our gaze from our only true reference, we become self-referential. We withdraw into a 'self' not created by God's desire, but a *self* constructed by our own reflected deception.

God, however, never distances nor withdraws himself from his creation. Jurgen Moltman speaks about the 'Shekinah' as God's self-distinction, whereby he can identify with and is present with His people in their fate.

> *God loves his creation. God is bound to every one of his creatures in passionate affirmation. God loves with creative love. That is why he himself dwells empathically in every created being, feeling himself into them by virtue of his love. The love draws him out of himself, so to speak, carrying him wholly into the created beings whom he*

loves. Because he is 'the lover of life', his eternal Spirit is 'in all things' as their vital force. In the self-distinction and the self-giving of love, God is present in all his creatures and is himself their innermost mystery. The moment a created being turns away from this divine love, from which it nevertheless lives, it becomes anxious, aggressive and destructive, because it becomes self-seeking. Its will cuts it off from God's will, and its life turns away from the love of God, to self-hate. The whole misery of men and women comes from a love for God that has miscarried. And the result is on God's side what Martin Buber called a 'de-selfing' (Entselbung) - a kind of self-emptying of God. His Shekinah indwells every one of his creatures; but this Shekinah is now alienated from God himself. It is grieved and hurt, but it does not leave these lost beings to themselves. It suffers in the victims and is tormented in the perpetrators. It goes with sinners on the wanderings of their estrangement. The Shekinah does not leave us. Even in our most frightful errors, it accompanies us with its great yearning for God, its homesickness to be one with God. We sense its pain in the 'drawing' of the Spirit. With every bit of self-seeking and self-contradiction which we surrender to the will of the Creator who loves us, the Shekinah comes close to God. If we live entirely in the prayer 'Thy will be done', the Shekinah in us is united with God himself. We live again wholly, and can undividedly affirm life. The wanderings are over. The goal has been

*reached. We are conscious of God's happiness in us, and
are conscious of ourselves in God's bliss.[4]*

If Jesus demonstrated anything, it is that God is deeply
involved and affected by our fallen world. Sin is not simply
something he is offended by, from a distance. He suffers
the consequences of our sin with us. He is tormented with
us, dies with us and even enters our hell with us. The fact
that this distance is caused by our deception does not make
the suffering less real.

In Mimetic Atonement, therefore, the distance is never
created or maintained by God, but rather it is a distance
created and maintained by our own deception. We were
alienated and enemies in our minds (Colossians 1:21).
The anguish of this separation is however experienced by
both man and God, for the One in whom all things exists
experiences everything with us. Atonement in this context
can only happen when we are delivered from this kingdom
of illusion. But if one is deceived, one does not know it,
otherwise it would not be deception. It therefore requires
that God take the initiative and break into our world
of shadows, through our blindness and into our hell of
confusion to bring His truth, His sight, His understanding
there.

---

4   Jurgen Moltmann. The Spirit of Life (Kindle Locations 775-790).
Kindle Edition.

RELATIONSHIP OF LAW AND SIN

Paul wrote that the Law is holy, just and good. Why? Because it is through the law that we learn what is prohibited. Its instruction and purpose was to bring life by keeping us from what was destructive, but its purpose was perverted to the extent that it brought death (Romans 7:7-13).

How did this perversion take place?

Whatever is prohibited, becomes more desirable.

If the desire within me intensifies, but I am prohibited from fulfilling it, internal conflict increases. And whether one succumbs to the temptation or not, the conflict remains unresolved. Twisted desire (sin), therefore, found opportunity within the Law of prohibition, to strengthen itself.

Laws of prohibition by themselves are good and just. There is nothing wrong with the command that says: you shall not steal or you shall not kill. But these laws by themselves are unable to transform the desires that give birth to these actions. In fact, the way in which desire functions means that these desires are stirred by the very laws that prohibit their expression.

Intentions or desires do not simply arise out of nothing, they are mimetic. In other words they are formed in relationship, suggested to us by others. We mirror the perceived intentions of others, some of these intentions we claim as our own, others we reject, but all of them come to us through the mirroring process. We have often personified evil as we projected evil outside ourselves into a form more easily identified and explained. However, the evil that enslaved humanity is not some external personality, but as Paul wrote, '*sin that dwells within me*' (Romans 7).

The Law, therefore, became the great accuser (Satanos). Its demands conflicted with our desires and caused internal conflict to the point Paul describes as internal death!

Why could the law not transform our desires?
Because desires are suggested to us by a model that is like us. We naturally reflect persons, not laws or abstract theories. It can only be the revelation of our true model, the light that enlightens every man, that transforms us into our true selves.

In Galatians 3 Paul argues further that God's actual purpose behind the law was a strategic phase in which we, like immature children, had to be subjected to the rule of a teacher. The time of maturity, in which we could be trusted to make wise decisions, came with Christ. It is the faith of Christ, the person of Christ, the desires of Christ, that awakens in us equivalent faith and desire. In encounter with Christ, we can once again be trusted to live from a desire and a faith that is naturally good.

WHAT IS MIMETIC ATONEMENT?

So what did Jesus accomplish?

What did his life, death and resurrection do for our world?

If the source of broken relationship was an offended God, then punishment equal to the offense would seem like the best solution. By broken relationship I mean the relationship between God and mankind, our relationships with each other, and our relationship with creation. However, we have identified many contradictions and weaknesses in the Penal Substitution Theory of atonement. I maintain that God is not the problem we needed to be saved from.

If a very evil personality, named Satan, is the source of broken relationship, then his utter defeat would solve the problem. The presence of suffering and evil in this world would suggest that, either he was not utterly defeated and Jesus failed in his mission according to 1 John 3:8, or the personified view of Satan is incorrect.

If the source of this disharmony between ourselves, ourselves and God, and ourselves and creation, is our own inherent blindness, then harmonious at-one-ment involves the kind of revelation that shatters our isolating illusions and reveals us as located in the bosom of our Abba. It is the kind of revelation that inspires the words found in Psalms 17:15 "*As for me, I will behold thy face in righteousness: I shall be satisfied, when I awake, with thy likeness.*"

The very nature of atonement is revelation.[5] In the same way in which our blindness was more than wrong beliefs, so this revelation is more than accepting right beliefs. What we fundamentally believe about ourselves, about others and about God, cannot be changed by simply being presented with new information.

Humanity's inherent blindness is the result of a formative event in our past. The revelation of Jesus Christ is a new formative event that introduces a divine idea into the human constitution. These formative events do not happen on an intellectual level to begin with, but on the level of desire - the unconscious movements that bring consciousness into being.

Mimetic revelation is the encounter in which every desire I have allowed to form me dissolves, and consequently I am undone. It is the event in which I am re-formed as I come face to face with my origin, the authentic desire that imagined me and brought me forth, the God who is love. The boundaries of who I think I am disintegrate when I realize that love defines me.

Revelation is both a destructive and constructive event. It has the power to obliterate illusions and uncover the beauty of reality in the same event. In Jesus, God and man encounter one another in direct mimetic reflection. It is

---

5   Romans 1:16,17, Galations 1:15,16; 3:2, 1 Corinthians 2:9,10

the event in which the unconscious grip of myth is broken from our collective consciousness and simultaneously the moment in which the beauty of God's love for us shines most clearly.

The life, death and resurrection of Jesus is God's self revelation within our history and, as such, atonement is a historic event. But atonement is also more than history, it is the "now" or "wow" moment in which the Spirit of God opens my eyes to see the true God and find myself as his reflection. This Spirit is the Spirit of Christ, meaning that just as Christ Jesus concluded human history in his death and transformed human destiny through his resurrection, so the Spirit of Christ concludes my life story and then makes all things new.

THE DEPTH OF HIS IDENTIFICATION

How can such a revelation be accomplished? Does God send us a written account of truth? Does he persuade us through rational argument? Truth might be glimpsed at through scripture and grasped at through conversation, but ultimately it can only be encountered in likeness. As reflective beings we are most deeply impacted by one like ourselves and so the word became flesh; the truth became one with us so that we may become true in relationship with him.

This likeness has a double movement. Firstly, for us to recognize Christ as one like ourselves, he needs to enter fully into our human condition. It is only what he becomes that can be reached and saved. For only if we perceive a God fully like us, are we able to believe that we can be like him. He needs to demonstrate to what extent he understands and mirrors us. This identification, this solidarity, needs to be with all humanity in order to be relevant to all humanity.

Consequently, we see the way in which Jesus recapitulates[6] all of human history. His identification with the outcasts, the victims, demonstrates his solidarity with our suffering. This takes his life beyond the boundaries of simply a good moral example. It is decidedly more.

The incarnation is not the first time that God experiences what it is like to be human. All things consist in him (Colossians 1:17) and he sustains all things in existence through the word of his power (Hebrews 1:3). There is not one experience any person has ever had, that God did not experience with them. He understands us better than we understand ourselves. The incarnation is the first time that we come to know *that God knows* what it is like to be human. This identification grows and reaches its crescendo in the cross.

---

6   recapitulate: to summarize and state again the main points

When on that cross he cries out: *"Elí, Elí, lemáa sabachtháni?" that is, "My God, My God, why have You forsaken Me?"*, he enters into the depth of human despair. Jesus, as fully human, takes upon himself the mindset of alienated humanity and cries out what we have felt.

This is the moment where the omnipotent God experiences what it is like to be helpless and forsaken.
The immortal God faces death.
Here we see the Omniscient One experiencing our confusion.
He partakes even of our doubt... so that we might become partakers of his faith.

But this is only the first of a double movement of mimetic identification. Secondly, now that we know that he understands, now that we see the depth of his commitment to us, now that he has our attention, he reveals our authentic humanity. It is now our turn to identify with him. His life up to and including his death reveals that he knows what it is like to be a victim and as such he also understands the perpetrators of evil. But his solidarity with us, although it may bring comfort, does not by itself change the victims or perpetrators. The resurrection is the event that breaks through this cycle of victimage and exploitation. He demonstrates to us that the victim can do more than hope for revenge - the victim can forgive and so become something completely new. Similarly, victimizers seeing themselves clearly for the first time in the one they murdered are immediately shown something more: Their resurrected victim forgives them and so gives them an opportunity to transcend themselves, to be justified and given a whole new way of being human. The One who is like us models a new way of being human, opening up new possibilities of being. Now that we know how much like us he is, he demonstrates what God imagines humanity to be: self-giving lovers, just like himself.

THE NECESSITY OF THE CROSS

So what necessitates the cross? If God does not delight in, neither requires, the violence of the cross to satisfy a need for retribution, then what did necessitate the cross? I want to offer a summary of four interwoven reasons for this brutal death:

1. In Jesus' own words, the reason for his life was not death, but resurrection!

> *Jesus began to show his disciples that he must go to Jerusalem and suffer many things from the elders and chief priests and scribes, and be killed, and on the third day be raised."*
> (Matthew 16:21 ESV)
> *...and they will kill him, and he will be raised on the third day.*
> (Matthew 17:23 ESV)

(See also Matthew 17:9,23, 20:19, 26:32, Mark 14:28, Luke 9:22)

Jesus understood his ultimate redemptive mission, not as sacrificial death, but resurrection life. It is, therefore, the resurrection that necessitates his death. He had to die because he was destined to overcome death with resurrection life.

2. As we've seen in the previous section, it was necessary for him to identify with man to the deepest extent, for it is only what he becomes that is saved, only what he assumes that is healed. It is by being wounded, that he heals us. As such he had to become us, in our most dreadful state, in our most helpless condition, in our deepest fear and confusion. It is because he became all that we are, that we can be all he is, which brings us to the next reason.

3. He becomes all we are so that the victory he achieves is not the victory of an almighty God over an evil arch enemy. But as fully human, he faces our fear on our behalf and conquers it. The image of a God threatening us with death as punishment, is overthrown with the image of a God who would rather suffer with us than inflict suffering on us. If God is the only one worth fearing and we need not fear him, then nothing is worth fearing. Consequently,

he delivers *all those who through fear of death were subject to lifelong slavery.*[7]

The most fundamental fear, the human sense of inadequacy that caused Adam and Eve to grasp at attaining the likeness of God, is brilliantly ambushed by Jesus, who being in *the form of God, did not count equality with God a thing to be grasped, but emptied himself, by taking the form of a servant, being born in the likeness of men.*[8] He fully invests himself into human form and is fully satisfied with being human. This state of being does not leave him with a sense of lack or emptiness, but he demonstrates that all the fullness of God is at home in the human body (Col 2:8-10). It is this sense of completeness, this deep persuasion that God is satisfied with our humanity, that gives Jesus the strength not to bow to fear, not to accept the pressure of the crowd, but to have the courage to simply be human without shame... even in the face of the most humiliating death.

4. It was in the act of blind rage that the single victim mechanism was born. The brutality of murdering one of our own became the sacrificial system with which violence was controlled. The religions born from these sacrificial rituals, the myths that grew from them, the societies we built upon sacred violence and the vengeful god-images we nourished through this event, made it the only relevant

---

7   Hebrews 2:15 ESV

8   Philippians 2:6–7 ESV

event by which to subvert this human wisdom. It had to be the cross that was the undoing of systematic violence, for the cross was the ultimate sign of domination, the symbol of a system that does not recognize individual value in its pursuit for social order.

So we can conclude that the cross was necessary *for us*, to open our eyes, to expose evil and reveal an Abba that fully accepts us. The only way in which it was necessary for God, was in its necessity for us to come to our senses. To save us from our violence, he was willing to endure the violent cross. To save us from the fear of death, he faced the horror of it for us. For the joy of restored relationship he endured the sorrow, the shame, and the isolation of the cross.

SACRIFICE SUBVERTED

Jesus so radically subverted sacrifice, that the practice of it stops wherever the gospel is heard and embraced. The violence that leads to the practice of sacrifice and the retributive gods born from it, are all exposed for what they really are: our own misplaced fears and insecurities.

Jesus not only brings the old practice of sacrifice to an end, he also transforms the very concept. We sacrificed others for our own benefit - divine sacrifice is the self-giving love with which we benefit others. Human sacrifice fused and therefore confused violence and the sacred - Jesus' sacrifice reveals that our violence is our own and God's goodness is pure and free.

So in what way was Jesus' sacrifice the perfect, once and for all, sacrifice? Well, what would be the perfect sacrifice for a God who says: "*Sacrifices and offerings I have not required*"? Would it not be the sacrifice that forever and finally ends the practice of sacrifice by exposing its deceptive nature?

According to Hebrews 10, the very concept that sacrifice purges us from sin was part of its weakness. On this basis, a clear conscience was dependent on continually re-enacting the ritual. God desired for man's conscience to be perfected, that is, no longer subject to the debilitating bondage of sin and guilt. How can our conscience possibly be perfected? Certainly not by convincing ourselves that nothing is wrong, or worse, that nothing was ever wrong! Rather, it is by entering the sobering and clear revelation of what man is without God, what evil is, and at the same time coming face to face with God himself - our true reference. In this encounter he takes the initiative to *put his laws on our hearts, and write them on our minds.*[9] The sacrifice of Jesus did not change God's mind about us, but rather changes our understanding of God and ourselves.

...justification comes "through the redemption [the ransoming or buying back] that is in Christ Jesus, whom

---

9   Hebrews 10:16 ESV

God put forward as a sacrifice of atonement by his blood, effective through faith." How are we to take the phrase "as a sacrifice of atonement"? Is this a specification of the heart of God's purpose, or is it a description of a position, a place taken up by Christ in the service of God's purpose to redeem and ransom humanity? I incline to the latter. God enters into the position of the victim of sacrificial atonement (a position already defined by human practice) and occupies it so as to be able to act from that place to reverse sacrifice and redeem us from it. God steps forward in Jesus to be one subject to the human practice of atonement in blood, not because that is God's preferred logic or because this itself is God's aim, but because this is the very site where human bondage and sin are enacted. God "puts forward" the divine Word into this location as part of the larger purpose of ransom, of transforming the situation from within. The text immediately points out that the effectiveness of this act lies not in the blood or the violence; it relates to faith."[10]

The concept of sacrifice is therefore subverted. It can no longer be seen as a way to manipulate a reluctant God, a way to change God's disposition to be more favorable to us. Rather, the perfect sacrifice gives himself freely in the knowledge that God is pleased - that he is the beloved son. We can no longer sacrifice others or ourselves, thinking

10   Mark S. Heim. Saved from Sacrifice: A Theology of the Cross (Kindle Locations 1949-1956). Kindle Edition.

that this is what God requires from us to make him happy. Rather, because we are embraced by a happy God, we can freely give ourselves for the benefit of others, just as our model did.

Does Forgiveness Require Blood?

In the context of this teaching on sacrifice, we are often asked: *"Doesn't the bible say that without the shedding of blood there is no forgiveness of sins?"*

Well that's not exactly what it says. Let's look at Heb 9:22:

"According to the law almost everything is purified with blood, and without the shedding of blood there is no forgiveness."

First point to notice: *"According to the law"*
Many things that were introduced by the law only find their full and final meaning in Christ. The book of Hebrews is focused on helping people who were totally invested in the old understanding of law and sacrifice, to see beyond the shadows and types and realize its true meaning. As such the sacrificial system was only a type: God spoke to us in sacrificial language because that is what we could understand, but he brought that conversation to a final conclusion in the perfect sacrifice. He is the perfect sacrifice, because he is the first *real* sacrifice: a self-sacrifice for the benefit of others. Similarly, Jesus fulfills the law not by

meeting its every requirement, but by bringing its shadows to an end in the light of the resurrection.

The second point to notice is: "... **almost** *everything is purified by the blood*".
That little word "almost" becomes very problematic if one thinks that blood is the only substance containing the magical qualities necessary to enable forgiveness. That is also why the whole verse is often not quoted, so that the phrases "according to the law" and "almost everything" can be avoided.

The background to this verse is the Levitical sacrificial system. The amazing thing about the Levitical requirements for atoning sacrifices is that they did not always require blood! (Lev 4:1-6:7) If a person was too poor to afford the usual sacrifice, then a grain offering was accepted. God was not going to allow blood to stand between his desire to forgive and a person in need of forgiveness! So then, even under the law, blood was not always required as a prerequisite for forgiveness.

And now his blood speaks of better things than the blood of Abel (Heb 12:24). The blood of all innocent victims, since Abel, called for vengeance, called for retributive justice. Unfortunately, we have often reduced the message of the blood of Christ to speak the same message as Abel's blood when we referred to it as the blood God required to enable him to forgive sins. No! His blood has a better message – his blood calls for forgiveness not vengeance! This is why his blood purifies our conscience – it communicates God's absolute, unreserved forgiveness even while we were at enmity against him.

God's forgiveness is indeed utterly and completely freely given, not in exchange for anything, but in his own freedom and by his own initiative. In this too he acts as our model, enabling us to transcend our retributive history.

17 - BEAUTIFUL CONTRASTS

There are so many ideas about God and man. Some ideas are beautiful... some are monstrous... all are subjective. All our ideas are subject to influences we are not even conscious of.

Is there any way to break through the limitations of our own understanding? Are we doomed to forever worship our own projections, our own imagined reflections, gods created in our own image and likeness?

... or is there a knowledge that does not originate in ourselves?

... can we hear a word that is not the word of another man, but a resonance with a sound that is utterly other, yet strangely familiar?

... are we able to recognize likeness, not just among ourselves, but with that which was from the beginning, the Word that was and is God?

Every attempt of man to know and describe God has proven to be utterly futile. The only possible way to know God is if he takes the initiative to make himself known.

The Word that became flesh is God's initiative to reveal himself and to deliver us from ourselves. He came to deliver us from our own imaginations, the circular reflections in which we were caught with no way out. He came to break the perverted mimetic cycle in which we had nothing but one another's confusion to reflect. Victims and victimizers were endlessly recycled with the pain and injustice simply taking different forms. Salvation is nothing less that God taking the initiative to break this hypnotic cycle by revealing himself. Let's now explore the beauty and mystery of God's self-revelation through Jesus Christ.

MYSTERY OR ABSURDITY?

What is the difference between mystery and absurdity? Complex ideas have many intricate connections. Two concepts might each be true in themselves but seem to state the logical opposite from the other. Attempting to reconcile such seemingly contradictory statements can result in either a beautiful mystery or an absurdity. Avoiding the task of reconciling them and simply accepting each one as true, means that our understanding of their truth will remain shallow, disconnected and confused. Alternatively, if one attempts to reconcile them by restating them in such a way that they both say the same thing, then reconciliation has failed! Simply removing all contradictions from both concepts, and only retaining their similarities, is to demean both of them. Such 're-statements' reduce the concepts to meaningless sameness and are simply ridiculous.

Reconciling true yet opposing concepts, means that we honor their distinctions and simultaneously recognize their points of agreement. In understanding both distinction and similarity we are able to bring such concepts into peaceful relationship. The differences are held in tension because a deeper connection is understood. This is the beauty of mystery.

A simple yet profound example is marriage. After more than 24 years of marriage, Mary-Anne and I have more in common than ever before, yet, paradoxically, our differences are also more apparent than ever. It is both the differences and the similarities that make relationship exciting and living. What a delightful mystery: union, yet distinction; intimate nearness, yet distance. It is the distance that creates space for relationship. In this relationship, desire finds tangible fulfillment, yet is ever awakened anew in the distance that remains. Let's now look at a few of these mysteries as they relate to God.

IMMANENCE AND TRANSCENDENCE

How can God be both immanent and transcendent, near and distant, intimately present, yet infinitely beyond all we know? Let's first explore the truth of each of these statements.

God's immanence is his immediate presence, availability and nearness in all of creation. He is the breath of every living thing[1] and all of creation pours forth his voice[2]. All things are held together by him[3] and nothing exists except through him[4]. He is therefore revealed in all that is. The most perfect example of this is the word made flesh, Jesus Christ, who is the exact representation of the nature and character of God.[5]

God's transcendence, on the other hand, is his absolute difference, his infinite distance from creation[6]. He is the source and the reason for all existence, but is not the same as anything that exists. As such, knowledge of him cannot be reduced to anything natural. God does not exist as a being among other beings. The infinite cannot be defined. To experience God is to experience the failure of our own intellect as we are confronted by the inconceivable, a reality much greater than the boundaries of our minds,[7] a peace that surpasses understanding (Phil 4:9). It is only in this place of acknowledging the failure of our intellect

---

1   Job 12:10
2   Psalm 19
3   Colossians 1:17
4   1 Corinthians 8:6
5   Hebrews 1:3
6   John 1:1-3
7   1 Corinthians 2:9

to contain God, that intellect can begin to fulfill its part in participating in an experience greater than itself.

So how can both these concepts be true? What do they have in common? Well, we can say that God is present and available, but is also beyond the present in the unimaginable. He is revealed in all of creation, yet what can be known of God is not exhausted by this revelation… much still remains unknown. Equally true, what remains unknown does not nullify what is revealed. God validates the message and person of Jesus by raising him from the dead. In this unparalleled event God has unveiled his nature and character like nowhere else… but it is an event and a revelation that continually unfolds. It gives access into God's infinity which, by definition, will remain more than we can ever explore.

OTHERNESS AND LIKENESS

'Otherness' and 'likeness' are obviously related concepts to immanence and transcendence. However, they are of particular relevance to mankind's relationship with God as creatures made in his image and likeness.

Otherness can be frightening and dangerous for it represents the unknown. We want enough otherness to intrigue us, but not so much as to scare us. Otherness, because it is unknown, has the potential to harm us.

Likeness can be frightening and dangerous too, for if someone is too much like me, they can replace me. As such, likeness can represent the disintegration of differentiation. When boundaries disintegrate it makes us uncomfortable. We want enough likeness to be comfortably familiar, but not too much likeness so as to lose our sense of uniqueness. Equality has the potential to eliminate us.

Despite these potential dangers, love is only possible when both likeness and otherness are present. God is the most surprisingly beautiful encounter with otherness and likeness one can ever have.

If the otherness of God is emphasized, without an appreciation of likeness, then God becomes only unknowable, unapproachable, unpredictable. In short, he is to be avoided. This is the kind of otherness in which there is no place for likeness, an otherness that can only be feared, not loved.

Now there is undoubtedly something very surprising, something very other about the God revealed in Jesus. He is beyond what we have ever imagined, but at the same time he is the God who delights in revealing himself, not in withdrawing into utter unknowability.

How can God remain other yet reveal himself? Well there is so much to be revealed! He is not unknown because he hides himself, but because the revelation of who he is will never be exhausted. In Jesus, the most essential quality of God is revealed: God is love and what we do not know about him yet, does not nullify what we do know. Jesus surprises us with a God who is more like us than what we ever imagined; a God who defines himself as God-with-us. He will never again be God-without-us. In Jesus we recognize God as flesh of our flesh and bone of our bone. This likeness is an opportunity to reflect the adoration he gives us. The God revealed in Jesus is so much like us that He does not flinch from becoming our equal! But this is not an equality that will produce competition, for distinction remains. This is an equality that makes the highest level of fellowship possible – a fellowship in which we share in the divine nature.

Yet he never becomes ordinary. He remains *other* in that he continues to overwhelm us with an ever new love, continually unfolding in fresh and unexpected ways. Encountering God remains an astonishing event, no matter how often we have experienced it. In the context of relationship, God has always been and will always be unexpected, astonishing, exciting and surprisingly *other*. The only thing about God that is predictable is love, but even his love finds expression in the most unusual ways.

Whenever God becomes boringly predictable, you are busy with your own finite ideas about God, not with God himself. No matter how intense your experiences of God have been, there remains more to be experienced and surprised by.

In summary, God's otherness is not dangerous and therefore it is not to be feared for what we know beyond doubt is that God is love. His otherness is the exciting infinite possibility to be surprised by a God who is better than what we've ever imagined. His otherness means we can never get bored with him!

God is both surprisingly other and invitingly like us. The mystery of love is experienced in the paradox of otherness and likeness simultaneously present. The space between them is filled with creative movement. To love is God's freedom. To love is God's justice. To love in new and surprising ways, is God's creativity.

This is why you are here! The love within the Godhead is the love of 'like' for 'like' within himself. In God's freedom, he wanted to extend this love to *likeness* within *another*. "*And Elohim said: Let us make man in our image and likeness.*"

In creation God expressed himself beyond himself. So although creation is intimately upheld and sustained by him, it is 'other' from him. Creation and the Creator are not one and the same, they are distinct. This does not mean that he is removed, uninvolved or not present in creation.

On the contrary, Jesus reveals a God who is here, who is more intimately involved than what we ever imagined, more present than what we are aware of. Yet, he remains distinct... and it is this very distinction that makes romance possible. In creation and specifically in man, the love of God finds opportunity to flow beyond the Godhead. It has freedom to be expressed to another... even towards the extreme other - towards enemies.

CHANGELESS AND TEMPORAL

Another such mystery is God's changeless yet temporal nature. Stating that God is changeless is for most believers a no-brainer. In a world of constant change and insecurity, it is comforting to conceive of God as changeless. And indeed God's faithfulness, his eternal steadfastness, his unending mercies, are testified to throughout the scriptures.

Early Christianity's dialogue with Hellenistic philosophy did much to strengthen a particular view of God's changelessness. Plato's ideas of eternity, in which the perfect, changeless and true form of everything exists, influenced the way in which they conceived of God. In the context of these philosophies, God became the eternal, perfect, changeless one. Although this view was disputed from the beginning, the doctrine of God's impassibility soon became standard teaching. Impassibility basically means: not able to suffer, experience emotion or be changed in any way.

But does *changeless* not also mean, boring sameness? If God is absolutely changeless, then how can he have any empathy for our existence?

God's temporality, on the other hand, is his intimate involvement in our world. Nowhere was this revealed more clearly than in the suffering, temptation, pain, sorrow, injustice and death of Christ. *"For because he himself has suffered when tempted, he is able to help those who are being tempted"* (Hebrews 2:18 ESV). God has demonstrated in the most convincing way that he understands us deeply, for there is nothing we experience that he does not experience with us. The incarnation is God's declaration that he is completely invested in our humanity. He has bound himself inseparably to our existence, and as such he is deeply affected by humanity.

How can both be true?
How can a God who changes be trusted?
How can a God who remains unmoved by our suffering have empathy for?
Well, I think God himself would object to being described as boring sameness. The resurrection of Jesus reveals a God of infinite possibility, a God of unending surprise. So we can say that God's essential character, which is love, is unchanging. Even in the events in which we did our worst, utterly rejecting this love and murdering the Son of God, he remained faithful, forgiving and loving towards us.

Simultaneously we can say that God's changeless nature does not prevent him from experiencing the temporal with us.

TIME AND ETERNITY

Our concepts of time and eternity cannot be separated from our understanding of God's changeless and temporal character. In Hellenic thought, eternity is the motionless center of circling time; eternity is the unchangeable stable sameness in which we can ground all the moving things of our temporal realm. These philosophies frame the relationship between time and eternity rather negatively. Eternity becomes then, in many ways, the exact opposite of time.

Jesus, however, gives us a completely different picture of eternity and therefore of time. The God revealed in Jesus involves himself in our temporal world, he keeps things moving, he upholds all things by the word of his power (Heb 1:3), and in him all things consist (Col 1:17). This eternity is not the opposite of time, neither is it removed from time, but rather it fills and fulfills time. God's eternity is not motionless sameness, but rather it overcomes all sameness with infinite possibilities. Neither is it static timelessness, rather it is the dynamic movements within him that define eternity and sustain time. He moves faster than time and his eternity consists in exactly that: time itself will never exhaust God.

There is a context in which eternity can be described as timeless, but not timeless in the sense that it is the opposite of time and detached from time. Rather, time is birthed by eternity - time is the created parallel to the uncreated movements in God. However, within this created realm we have been given freedom to participate in these movements.

Scripture reveals a God who, even before creation and therefore before time, was active in giving and receiving, dynamic in relationship, choosing and calling, plotting and planning[8], active in acts of grace and salvation[9]. The scriptures testify to a God who needs nothing[10], a God who does not grow weary or tired[11], a God who is full and complete in himself. And yet he is a God who from the very beginning has been entangled in a love that is dynamic, moving, giving and ever finding new avenues of expression[12].

Eternity is the very relationship between Father, Son and Spirit. He is within himself the creative origin, the creative process and the artistic end result of his own creative genius. The movements within God - the fellowship, the creativity, the intentions, the witnessing, the breathing - these are the dynamics that constitute eternity. Time was designed to prolong and intensify the joy and anticipation

8	Eph 1:4,9-11
9	2 Tim 1:9
10	Acts 17:25
11	Ps 121:4, Job 22:2
12	John 17:24

of this romance. The story within God had to be told. Creation is the book, and time is the story written in it.

If time is understood as movement and event, then eternity is not timeless, but rather uncreated time. For there was relationship and movement, even before creation - the Creator precedes creation. Whereas some philosophies see eternity as the ultimate escape into a timeless dimension, God's eternity is expressed in his faithfulness throughout time.

Our time, which became corrupted, fragile and broken apart into a regrettable past, an unsubstantial present and a fearful future, finds redemption in Jesus Christ. He comes to heal our memories, our awareness and our anticipation.

DESIRE FULFILLED AND AWAKENED ANEW

As Christians we have often been encouraged to hunger and thirst after God. And the logic seems sound: why would we pursue relationship with God if we had no desire for God? Yet, Jesus promises that *"whoever comes to me shall not hunger, and whoever believes in me shall never thirst"* (John 6:35 ESV).

So how can desire be fulfilled yet remain alive? How can God completely satisfy us, yet intrigue us and draw us toward greater fulfillment?

We have seen how desire, born from a sense of insufficiency, can cause all kinds of destruction and evil. Even a desire for God can become deadly if its source is a sense of lack of being. In Jesus, God demonstrates again that he does not withhold anything from us, but freely gives himself to us. He satisfies. Yet in this place of satisfaction, desire remains alive. In fact it is in this place of fullness that true desire is stirred.

We are intimately part of the interplay between beauty and desire. Beauty elusive, desire unquenched. Beauty plays, teases, and then gives itself wholly. It is in this self-giving that our eyes are opened to a beauty not seen before, a possibility not yet imagined. And so it is in the moment of overwhelming fullness that desire is awakened afresh and so the dance continues.

The beauty that awakens our hearts, that makes us alive, finds resonance within us, while simultaneously drawing us beyond ourselves. The space between what we are and what we could be is no longer the accusing, death-breath of obligation. No. We are satisfied with the being we have, yet the unrealized possibility of being beckons us to transcend ourselves.

There is a space, a distance, between what we are and the infinite possibility of being. Without this space we would only be stagnant, boring... a past that remains in the present. But there is a life-giving space, a joyful distance in which desire dwells, allowing what is, to touch what could be, wooing the present to shed its past and discover a future unbound. Desire dwells in this space between, the movement of ever-drawing-closer.

I am the stirring in your being,
the elusive beauty beyond,
and the space between.

I am no stagnant destination,
a statement confined,
a concept defined,
but the path, the living story,
the narrative unending.

I am what happens, when you
recognize the mystery in the music,
the silence, the sounds,
the crescendo to come.

I am the gift of distance,
the awareness of presence,
elusive and self-giving
evading and overwhelming.

I am no thing,
the infinite possibility
of everything.

I am who desires you,
although I have no need of you.

RECOMMENDED READING

Roughly organized by relevance to chapter

2. More Than Myself

- Mimesis and Science: Empirical Research on Imitation and the Mimetic Theory of Culture and Religion (Studies in Violence, Mimesis, & Culture), Michigan State University Press, Garrels, Scott R. (Editor),

- The Imitative Mind. Edited by Andrew N The Imitative Mind: Development, Evolution and Brain Bases (Cambridge Studies in Cognitive and Perceptual Development), Cambridge University Press, By Andrew N. Meltzoff (Editor), Wolfgang Prinz (Editor)

- Self Comes to Mind: Constructing the Conscious Brain, By Antonio Damasio

- Rene Girard and Creative Mimesis. By Thomas Ryba (Editor), Pablo Bandera (Contributor), Christina Biava (Contributor), & 14 more

3. Desire Found Me

- The Genesis of Desire (Studies in Violence, Mimesis, & Culture), By Jean-Michel Oughourlian

- The Lost World of Genesis One: Ancient Cosmology and the Origins Debate, By John H. Walton

- Understanding Genesis (The Heritage of Biblical Israel) By Nahum M. Sarna A Violent God-Image. Matthias Beier.

4. Desiring Your Neighbor's Ass

- The Scapegoat. By Rene Girard.
- Things Hidden from The Foundation of the World. By Rene Girard.
- The Prophetic Law: Essays in Judaism, Girardianism, Literary Studies, and the Ethical (Studies in Violence, Mimesis, & Culture), By Sandor Goodhart
- Evolution and Conversion: Dialogues on the Origins of Culture, By Girard, Rene; Joao Cezar de Castro; Antonello, Pierpaolo.

5. Reflective Language

- Time and Narrative. Volume 1. Paul Ricoeur
- An introduction to Rene Girard and Myth. Richard J Colsan.

6. Scripture Conversing with Myth

- Who Wrote the Bible? By Richard Elliot Friedman.
- Scribal Culture. By Karel Van Der Toorn.
- The Bible Tells Me So. By Peter Enns.
- The Human Faces of God, By Thom Stark

7. Mystery of God

- The Origins of Biblical Monotheism: Israel's Polytheistic Background and the Ugaritic Texts. By Mark S. Smith.
- The Memoirs of God. By Mark S. Smith
- The Experience of God. Being, Consciousness, Bliss. By David Bentley Hart.
- Did God Have a Wife. By William G. Dever
- Must There Be Scapegoats. By Raymund Schwager, SJ

8. Story of Sacrifice

- The Death and Resurrection of the Beloved Son, by Jon D. Leverson

9. Paradox of Evil

- Figuring the Sacred, Paul Ricoeur
- The Symbolism of Evil, Paul Ricoeur

10. History of Satan

- I see Satan Fall like Lightning, Rene Girard
- The Origin of Satan. Elaine Pagels.
- The Birth of Satan. T.J Wray and Gregory Mobley

11. Coming God

- The Coming God. Jurgen Moltmann.

12. History Summarized in His Story

- Jesus in the Drama of Salvation. Raymund Schwager.
- The Spirit of Life. Jurgen Moltmann.
- The Scapegoat. Rene Girard.
- Girard and Theology. Michael Kiran.
- The Jesus Driven Life: Reconnecting Humanity With Jesus, 2nd Edition Revised and Expanded, By Michael Hardin

13. Zombie Apocalypse

- Jesus Risen in Our Midst, Sandra M. Schneiders
- The Resurrection Effect, Anthony J. Kelly
- Violence, Desire, and the Sacred. by Scott Cowdell (Editor), Chris Fleming (Editor), Joel Hodge (Editor)

14. Structure of Evil ... Undone

- <u>Puppets of Desire. Jean-Michel Oughourlian</u>

15. Atonement Theories and Sacrifice

- <u>Stricken by God? Edited by Brad Jersak (Editor), Michael Hardin (Editor)</u>
- <u>The Nonviolent Atonement. J Danny Weaver.</u>
- <u>Healing the Gospel. Derek Flood.</u>

16. Mimetic At-One-Ment

- <u>Saved from Sacrifice. Mark Heim.</u>
- <u>Atonement, Justice, and Peace. Dario W Snyder Belousek</u>
- <u>The Evolution of Adam. Peter Enns</u>
- <u>The Joy of Being Wrong. James Alison</u>
- <u>Banished from Eden. Raymund Schwager, SJ</u>

MORE RESOURCES BY ANDRE & MARY-ANNE RABE CAN BE FOUND AT:

<u>alwaysloved.net</u>

Printed in the USA
CPSIA information can be obtained
at www.ICGtesting.com
LVHW012035041023
759988LV00011B/313